MW00577897

UNREAL FOR REAL

UNREAL FOR REAL

(TRUE-LIFE STORIES)

ADAM MARS

NEW FUTURE BOOKS - LOS ANGELES

Copyright © 2018 by Adam Mars

All rights reserved. No part of this book may be reproduced in any form or by any electronic or mechanical means, including information storage and retrieval systems, without permission in writing from the publisher, except by a reviewer, who may quote brief passages in a review. Scanning, uploading, and electronic distribution of this book or the facilitation of such without the permission of the publisher is prohibited.

First Edition 2018

Library of Congress Number: 2018907233
ISBN-13: 978-0-692-12184-9

Cover Illustrations: Seth Barnard
Cover Design: Seth Barnard and Adam Mars
Interior Design: Adam Mars

Photos: Courtesy of Adam Mars, except *Portrait of Mistress Lyra* by Michael Vegas

NEW FUTURE BOOKS
1620 Scott Ave.
Los Angeles, CA 90026
www.newfuturebooks.com

1 2 3 4 5 6 7 8 9 10

Printed in the United States of America

For Mom, Majesta, Alex, and Shane.

And you may ask yourself, well, how did I get here?

Talking Heads

These stories are based on true events. They are not works of pure nonfiction. Dialogue, characters, details, and places have been invented, changed, and altered for creative and protective purposes.

CONTENTS

BEST PARTY EVER

-1-

When I was twelve years old, I went to the best party of my life—and not just up until that point. I mean, as I type these words, *it was the best party of my life.* After thousands of hangovers, benders in Vegas with billionaires, backstage ragers with rock stars, five-star adventures in Europe, six toxic years of college, and a decade in Los Angeles, it's still the best. There's no Beatles-or-Rolling-Stones debate over this one.

It was the fall of seventh grade. My best friend, Shane Murphy, had recently moved back to the small coastal town of Laguna Beach, California. Shane and I were born a few weeks apart, and even though he was half-Asian and we shared no genes, he was my brother. Our fathers were the closest of friends and for the first years of our existence we were inseparable. After his parents split town in 1986, he began an extended tour of relatives' homes that sent him to many different schools over many years.

3

When Shane came home in 1992, he was different. Puberty blessed him with good looks and a bad attitude—traits that would help make him the most desirable boy at Thurston Middle School. His chiseled face had mastered the look of 'cocky but clueless' and he wore his long hair better than any teen rebel on TV. It also didn't hurt that his mother was dating the drummer of one of the biggest bands in the world and they lived in the only eight-acre mansion in town. A few weeks into the school year, everyone knew about Shane, about the band, and about the house. They also knew that I was his best friend—a title I was not prepared to maintain.

Prior to Shane's arrival, I was moderately popular at school; not an alpha, but I was allowed to breathe the same air as the cool surfer guys. More importantly, girls without severe vision problems were starting to take notice of me. My brief partnership with T-zone acne ended that year and my appearance improved as the oil fields dried up. On top of that, I had my first good hair cut: perfectly tailored on all sides without the use of a buzzer or a bowl. All these favorable developments came with disappointment because they had yet to net me an open-mouthed kiss and a girlfriend.

I was, however, my dysfunctional parents' dream come true. I excelled in school—most notably in art—and I stayed out of trouble. Like most juvenile delinquents, Shane lived by his own set of rules, rules that allowed him to skip school and stay out past curfew. While I knew Shane's path to failure was an unwise detour from my road to success, he clearly offered the quickest route to teenage girls.

I ditched my proper lifestyle and followed his lead immediately.

-2-

One Friday morning during recess, I was talking to some of my friends when Shane raced over with big news.

"My uncle is throwing a party at my house tonight! You guys wanna come?"

Shane's uncle, Russ Won, was a cross between Bruce Lee and Jeff Spicoli: a master of the social arts and the ringleader of Laguna's early '90s party scene. But more than that, he was our idol. He owned an extraordinary collection of CDs and *Playboy* magazines that he let us sample at our leisure. Learning about grunge records and Anna Nicole Smith's tits was better than learning about algebra, so naturally Uncle Russ' bachelor pad became our preferred place to ditch school.

Earlier that week, Shane's mom went to Europe to protect her boyfriend from groupies while Stone Temple Pilots toured their hit record. There must have been a shortage of trained monkeys in Orange County, because Uncle Russ was put in charge of Shane while they were gone. I imagined we might get a few complimentary surfing sessions out of his babysitting role, but Uncle Russ had other plans.

The prospect of a house party meant this was going to be a late-night event with adults, alcohol, and things we'd only seen on Cinemax. We couldn't have our parents pick us up at an event like this. We'd get grounded for life and Shane would get blacklisted by the PTA. This was a mandatory sleepover. Unfortunately, getting clearance to spend the night at the new kid's house was tricky stuff in middle school. If you didn't have hippies or winos for parents (I had both), you needed someone like Bill Clinton to broker that arrangement. So when Shane popped the question—"You guys wanna come?"—he was met with mostly long faces.

There was still a handful of boys that figured their guardians would welcome their absence for one night. Those guys were Anton Reed, Chris Brooks, Edgar Robbins, Seth Wilson, and Casey McGuire. They were all eighth-graders. And they were all bad.

-3-

By the end of the school day, Shane's big party made the gossip headlines. Even though kids our age were only a few years removed from parties at Chuck E. Cheese's, we thought we were ready for the big leagues. I started drinking beer that summer and went to several teen gatherings, so I was pretty confident I could handle whatever the night threw at me. My cockiness got soft in a hurry when Shane told me that Piper Purdy might come to the party.

Piper Purdy was my middle school dream crush. She was a beautiful girl, both inside and out, with a warm smile that could melt an igloo. Oh, and she also had boobies (big ones). Beside the fact that she was a prized eighth-grader and could've had any guy in school, I was pretty sure she wanted me. We'd talk at school and sometimes at night on the telephone. As those nightly calls became more routine, I got word from one of her friends that she thought I was hot, or cute, or whatever scrawny twelve-year-old boys are to thirteen-year-old babes. I should've been stoked out of my mind, but now I had to make a move and I didn't know how. She was an intimidating challenge for any make-out virgin.

After Shane broke the news about Piper, we got on the bus with the rest of our party crew and headed toward his house. I could feel the screws on my adolescent training wheels getting loose under the weight of expectation, so I took a seat next to Shane and tried to settle my junior nervous breakdown.

"Did Piper say she was *definitely* gonna come to the party, or that she *might* come?"

"She said she was *definitely* coming!"

"Oh...great," I whimpered as my balls raced to my stomach.

"Yeah, she came up to me after sixth period and told me she's gonna spend the night at her cousins' house so her parents won't find out. She said they're all going to cruise by around nine o'clock."

Piper had two cousins in high school who were super hot and would have no trouble getting into a party hosted by a horny man. I assumed that was probably Piper's strategy, but I was a little jealous that she gave Shane a detailed outline of her plans.

"You know I like her, right?"

"Yeah, you tell me *every day*, dude."

"Well, do you like her now?"

I knew the only thing standing in the way of Piper was our friendship. And that was almost as sacred as big boobies.

"No, I don't!"

"Well, would you hook up with her if you could?"

Shane's half-Asian eyes went full Asian. That was a yes.

"I mean, I won't if you don't want me to."

"Are you fucking kidding me? Shane, I *definitely* don't want you to!"

"Well, shit, man! Then you better hook up with her, 'cause if you don't, then I don't see why you'd be mad if I did. It wouldn't be fair to anyone."

Shane was trying to weasel me with some bro-code loophole. He knew I wasn't primed for a girl like Piper, but I couldn't give in.

"Fine! I *will*!" I shouted.

He didn't look too convinced.

-4-

The bus dropped us off near Shane's house. It was located high above a rolling hillside filled with avocado trees and thick grass. An old metal gate blocked the street-side entrance, which Shane wedged open enough for us to squeeze through. From there, seven adolescent boys walked the long snakelike driveway toward the main house, talking the whole way about girls and alcohol and hand jobs. These delicacies had become commonplace to most of the guys. While I had very little to contribute to the conversation, I hoped that I'd be a vocal leader when the night was over.

When we finally reached the main house, our PG-13 panel discussion was pleasantly interrupted by the presence of Uncle Russ' beat-up Toyota pickup and a dozen other cars covered in surf stickers and dents. We nearly jizzed our pants when we saw what was inside the cars: kegs...*lots* of kegs. The much talked-about, but never actually seen in the wild, keg of beer was a magical thing to kids who treated Mickey's 40-ounce bottles like precious jewels. Besides the ocean of beer, there were piles of tacky Hawaiian decorations, a selection of instruments, massive speakers, cases of booze, tons of snacks, and a four-foot dead pig. Even Stevie Wonder could've seen that these were not the fixings for an average get-together. No, this was going to be a rager.

As we all grunted like Beavis and Butthead clones, the mastermind behind that evening's spectacle appeared. Uncle Russ stood on the front steps dressed in his trademark Quicksilver tank top, black trunks, and flip flops. His stringy long hair and scruffy Fu Manchu beard decorated his suntanned face, which was frowning at the sight of seven party fouls drooling over his party favors.

"Don't even think about it, grommets!"

In surf lingo, a grommet is a bottom-feeding runt to

any adult who knows how to surf even remotely well. It's non-negotiable. You are a grommet until guys stop referring to you as a grommet. Since Uncle Russ was a respected member of the Laguna surf community and could guarantee that we never caught another wave within the city limits, we froze up and focused on our superior. Shane tried to play it cool despite Uncle Russ' obvious displeasure.

"Oh, hey, Russ! I invited a couple friends over for the party, like you said I could."

"Well, there's six kids with you, stupid. A couple is *two*."

An atomic bomb instantly appeared over the Wonka factory. I knew I had the best chance at getting a golden ticket, but the other five guys were fair game. Shane's budding reputation at school was hinging on this party. If the guys that would be sent home wanted to relegate Shane to the loser squad, it would mean sudden social death for the both of us. Fortunately, one of them wasn't ready to let that decision arise.

"Sir, we'll do anything if you let us stay," Anton spoke up from the back of the pack with his hand politely raised.

Uncle Russ rolled his eyes so hard he probably sprained a retina. He knew damn well that our presence at his party could land him in jail. But not too long before, Uncle Russ was just like us, and he didn't grow up to be some dream-crushing dork.

"You grommets start unloading all this stuff and I'll think about it."

-5-

I had the cold, dead pig's head in my hands. Chris, Casey, and Seth were cradling the other corners of the beast as we waddled inside. Now, despite its massive size, Shane's house was kind of a piece of shit. It was desperately in need of a remodel, roaming with every creepy-ass insect under the sun, and its powder blue paint job was inspired by a Mexican motel. Basically, it was the type of place Edward Scissorhands might stay at if he sublet his goth pad and vacationed on the coast.

However, the run-down nature of the house made it an ideal setting to stage a party that would've slaughtered a nicer residence. Uncle Russ' buddies transformed the cluttered living room into a proper music stage, adorned with Technicolor lights. The kitchen where Shane's mom typically prepared fruit smoothies was overrun by women in their mid-twenties making fruity vodka punch they called 'jungle juice.' Outside, the poolside patio became party central where we loaded the pig onto a massive rotating BBQ spit. Sadly, our successful poke only led to less eventful chores as Uncle Russ sent us about the entire property to perform a home makeover until the once-shabby building became a temporary substitute for Honolulu.

Before we could say *aloha*, we were informed that we would have to get our parents' permission if we wanted to spend the night. The golden ticket was melting in my hands. How could I tell my mom and dad that I was going to an all-night keg party when they didn't even let me drink soda after 8 p.m. in their own home?

-6-

We all sat Indian-style around a large phone in the middle
of Shane's mom's bedroom. It seemed like the least appropriate place to conduct such business, but there we were;
collectively arranged like preschoolers, getting ready to lie
our asses off to full-grown adults. Uncle Russ showed a lot
of heart when he tried to improve our odds by crafting a
tame story.

"Just tell your parents we're gonna watch movies and
eat pizza and go surfing in the morning. And if they start to
wig out, tell them I'm a librarian, or something professional," he said with a shrug.

It was an alibi some parents might buy. Uncle Russ
tossed a cordless phone to Edgar and watched him test his
luck. Edgar said little more than, "Yo! Can I spend the night
at my friend's house?" before his mom approved. The
phone was then passed around until everyone made contact with the lords of their dwellings. Not a single parent
made a stink. It was as if they were waiting for someone
to hold their kids hostage. I too hoped for such parental
indifference.

As I punched the keypad with my shaky fingers, I
prayed to God, Satan, or anyone who was monitoring my
life that my mom would answer the phone. Her name was
Patsy, and she was a patsy (noun: a person who is easily
swindled, deceived, coerced, persuaded, etc.; sucker). Yet,

when the dial tone clicked over to a real human, I heard my dad. He was no patsy. He was a black belt in bullshitting. Getting a lie past him was like trying to safely remove a hangnail with a chainsaw.

With my peers awaiting my safe passage to Partytown, I did my best to relay Uncle Russ' white lie as if it were true. My dad knew that Uncle Russ was underqualified to be a librarian, but maybe we would watch movies and eat pizza and go surfing while we were watching bands and drinking beer and going wild. Somewhere in the midst of my stuttering monologue, my dad cut me off.

"Son, a few years ago, Russ went surfing and ended up drunk in Ensenada and I had to go bail his ass out of jail with Shane's dad. Did you know that?"

"Uh, no, Dad...but I'm sure he's learned his lesson!"

I could hear his blood pressure rising with each word I said into the phone.

"Put Russ on the damn line," he grumbled.

I passed the phone to Uncle Russ and observed as my dad tore him several new assholes before hanging up.

"If anything happens to you tonight, your dad's going to kill me," Uncle Russ said in a tone that was lacking even a molecule of sarcasm.

"I'll be good, Uncle Russ. I promise!"

He sprained his other retina, then laid down the rules. With our fingers crossed tightly behind our backs, we all agreed that we would not drink alcohol, do drugs, have fun, or die. I felt like uncrossing my fingers at that point. There was a much scarier hormonal vice that was threatening to get the best of me: Piper Purdy.

-7-

It started as a mellow gathering. By 7 p.m., a few dozen members of Uncle Russ' inner circle were scattered about the poolside patio watching the sun dip beyond the dark canyon. Our crew was stationed on an elevated staircase above the pool where we studied the social tendencies of the elders: how they pumped the keg, how they puffed their cigarettes. These observations were fascinating. And then they were boring.

In the pre-cell phone era, you couldn't cure boredom with Vitamin Wi-Fi. So Shane headed down to the keg station where life seemed more enjoyable. As usual, I went where Shane went.

A scrappy keg master eventually noticed us loitering around his waist as he handed out foamy Coors Lights.

"What the hell do you grommets want?"

Shane didn't miss a beat.

"I want a brew, bro!"

A chorus of cackles erupted amongst everyone within ear range. Yet before embarrassment reduced us to weeping losers, Shane utilized a tool that he handled better than anyone I've ever witnessed. It's called name-dropping, and it went a little something like this.

"Hey, man, I'm Russ' nephew and my mom is dating the drummer of Stone Temple Pilots and this is his house, so hook it up or get lost."

The guy nearly choked on his tongue.

"House cup!" he hollered into the air and then handed Shane a king's chalice in the form of a cheap red cup and filled it to the brim.

I stepped up to the plate and called upon my deepest vocal range, which was barely a tenor.

"Uh, I'm with that kid."

"Another house cup!"

It was that simple. I pulled the beverage to my lips and stared up at my dumbfounded friends. Like horny fans at a Madonna concert, they descended upon Shane and me, pawing for a sip of the forbidden nectar.

"Easy there, guys! Just say you're friends with Uncle Russ' nephew and they'll hook you up," Shane said confidently, with a foam mustache unknowingly branded across his upper lip.

A few minutes later, we had all violated a key rule of our overnight contract and were gearing up to be multiple offenders. Shane noticed a blazing Bob Marley-sized joint nearby and name-dropped until it was in his possession. I was raised in a liberal household where the smell of marijuana was more common than fresh air, so I rebelled against my parents by *not* smoking pot. When the joint made its way around to me, I disappeared into the keg line and quickly filled up on another family tradition.

The sky was now dark and more age-appropriate guests swarmed the patio. My buddies looked completely at ease with the social situation, like their sole purpose in life was to get drunk and high with people twice their age.

On the other hand, I was beginning to think that five-foot-tall males with 10 p.m. bedtimes should not live in such habitats, and I wanted to go home.

Over by the patio railing was a secret staircase that connected to the driveway—a shortcut back to comfortable adolescence. Once I came upon the staircase and looked down the driveway, I saw a major road hazard. A single police car was parked near the front gate, the unmistakable lights and decals branded across the metal body. When you've never been busted by the cops, it's the scariest prospect in the world. Great white sharks turn to guppies when compared to pre-teen arrests.

"Bros! Dudes! The cops are here!" I shouted as I scurried back to my friends.

"No way, you spaz!" Shane said while my friends all scoffed.

"Yes way, you dick! There's a cop car just chilling outside the gate!"

A phonetically-induced buzzkill washed over my friends. Together, we hurried over to the patio railing to catch a glimpse of the devil on wheels. I pointed in its direction, but in its place was a group of people, and no cop car. Everyone heckled me for being paranoid and not being able to handle alcohol; then they recommended that I drink more beer to calm down, so I did.

In the midst of Beer #3, the three hottest girls in high school—Joni Novack, Alicia Brown, and Kim Davies—were spotted in the driveway and they wanted Shane to usher them inside. We had never communicated with *any* of these girls. To my knowledge, they only talked to pro surfers and drug dealers; but that didn't dissuade Shane from racing to their aid to break bread. The social implications were so monumental that he brought Chris and me along to authenticate the encounter.

When we reached the driveway, the girls, dressed in skin-tight jeans and revealing tops, were standing by Uncle Russ' truck, flaunting like females who clearly lost their hymens.

"Hey, ladies! Welcome to *my* party!" Shane said, then flicked his hair to one side and pouted his lips.

I wondered if they even knew who Shane was prior to this nauseating exchange, but they cozied up to him as if they all came over on the *Mayflower*.

"Will you protect us if any old bitches try to kick us out for making them look ugly?" Alicia asked while her caked eyelashes fluttered. "They always start shit 'cause their boyfriends want to hook up with us."

"I'll kick *them* out if they say anything to you," he replied.

The girls squealed in unison when they realized they were granted diplomatic slutty immunity. Now that Shane had an assortment of arm candy, he strutted through the living room and left Chris and me to ride his coattails. A local punk band called the Surf Addicts was rocking out to a sizable crowd, which was my first experience with non-middle-school dancing. People were bouncing around and shaking their asses against a recipient's genital region. It looked like a pleasurable fusion of moshing and R.

Kelly's "Bump n' Grind" thrusting. When Shane started mimicking these moves on his tripod of babes, I figured he couldn't possibly handle *all* of them. After all, I was Shane's best friend, and in my newly intoxicated mind I embraced the potential benefits of such status.

At the end of one song, I turned to Kim Davies and boasted, "I'm Shane's best friend, and his Uncle Russ is throwing this party, and his mom is dating the drummer of Stone Temple Pilots, and this is *his* house."

Her eyes wanted to punch me. My first attempt at name-dropping failed to highlight me as the star of any of the desirable descriptions. Kim Davies wasn't going to waste her time on a glorified extra. She needed a leading male, or a pro surfer, or a drug dealer.

My unanimous rejection alerted me that I was getting too drunk for female interactions. I could live with Kim Davies' cold shoulder, but if I happened to rub Piper Purdy the wrong way, I'd be pissed off until Hell froze over. Food seemed to be the only antidote, so I headed outside and began nervously stuffing my face with Hawaiian buffet. It was almost 9 p.m.—the hour of Piper's reported arrival—when Uncle Russ caught me pulling pork off the rotating pig with my bare hands.

"Adam, you gotta be shitting me! Are you high?"

"No. Never. You said I couldn't, Uncle Russ."

My voice was not very good at telling the truth.

"I knew it! Now, back away from the animal and sober up, you stoned Wheat Thin!"

"But that's what I was trying to do!"

"What did you say?"

Despite all the pork I was chewing, my foot somehow found its way into my mouth.

"I said, 'I'll go drink a Mountain Dew.'"

"That's more like it, grommet."

I squeezed through a herd of drunks to reach the kitchen. A velvet rope eight acres long should've been strung across the property, but people kept cramming into every available nook. The Surf Addicts just finished their set and a young reggae band was preparing to make the herd sway again, so I grabbed a soda from the fridge and nudged my way into the living room to get a better view. What caught my eye was sweeter than Mountain Dew.

Piper Purdy stood near the front of the idle dance floor wearing smooth bell-bottom jeans with a matching jean jacket. She looked like some retro goddess from *Dazed and Confused*, but in my eyes she was Cassandra from *Wayne's World* shimmering in stardust while "Dream Weaver" blasted in my ears. As I overdosed on her teenage perfection, I began projecting a long, romantic future together: off campus lunches at Taco Bell and make-out sessions at my house while we watched *Beverly Hills 90210*. The fantasy dream world of Piper and Adam was a magical place I wanted to live in forever, or at least until Shane walked into frame and fucked it all up.

My slippery best friend arrived at Plymouth Rock before I did. He was noticeably without his posse of poontang when he greeted Piper with a hug. It was the kind of hug that only teenagers give: long, drawn out, and a physical stand-in for the sex we hadn't experienced. This was war. Piper wasn't my target anymore; Shane was. But Shane wasn't going to surrender easily. Why would he? He was Russ' nephew, and his mom was dating the drummer of Stone Temple Pilots, and this was *his* house.

With the odds against me, I fixed my hair, stood as tall as gravity would allow me, chucked my uncool soda on the ground, and walked up to Piper and the enemy.

"Hi!" I said to Piper, then craned around to Shane with a scowl so electric astronauts could see it from space.

"Piper, come with me and let me show you *my* house," Shane mumbled.

My scowl couldn't penetrate his atmosphere. He was way too stoned. I had to think of a diversion, fast.

"Um, Shane, I forgot to tell you, but Joni Novack is looking for you."

"She is? *Where*?"

I imagined the most distant location in the house.

"She's upstairs in the back bedroom. The *waaaaay* back part of the room. You should probably hurry before she's not there anymore."

Shane moved forward, ready to hunt down an upper-classman, but he caught a glimpse of Piper's plump cleavage and stopped on a dime.

"Actually, I think I'll hang here for a while," he said.

Curse big boobies and all the pain they cause!, I thought to myself.

"Isn't Joni that totally slutty ninth-grader?" Piper asked.

Shane disappeared faster than you could say 'teen pregnancy.'

"Wow. He's really wasted," Piper said with a laugh.

"Yeah, Shane's obviously not boyfriend material," I responded seriously.

"What do you mean?"

My explanation required a very large bus to throw him under.

"Nothing. Hey, do you want a beer?"

"Wow! Do you really think we can get one?"

"Yeah, this is practically *my* party."

Piper shot me a warm smile, then followed me to the kegs. Somewhere along the crowded route, I offered my hand to keep her on course. Piper clamped down, then continued with a flirtatious squeeze. Surprisingly, a courtesy gesture became my smoothest move on record. I had never held a hot girl's hand. I quickly learned they're called 'hot' because you literally heat up when you hold them. My palm became a nervous, soggy mess, and by the time we reached the kegs, I was clinging to Piper by the cells of my fingertips. Thankfully, I needed two clammy hands to grab our beers, so I swiftly disengaged before entering the beverage line. If I didn't ingest the confidence-building nutrients in alcohol fast, I'd surely lose Piper when Shane returned from his wild goose chase. The adults in front of me weren't helping my pursuit of romance. They nudged my puny body aside whenever I tried to cut in front of them.

As the physical impossibilities of getting beer became

apparent, I looked back at Piper and gave her a limp thumbs-up. To think I could satisfy anyone of the opposite sex at that age was proof that I was also the carrier of my mother's sucker gene. But one man's pain can quickly become a dumb boy's pleasure. A fistfight broke out by the pool and the keg line dispersed to watch some guy get pummeled. The ghost of Adolph Coors, the late beer company founder, was pulling strings from Heaven, enabling me to get some suds. So I grabbed the abandoned beer nozzle and started filling up two dirty cups I scrounged off the floor. The fight only lasted a few punches, but when the Grommet Police came back to reclaim their keg I had successfully hijacked one and a half cups of liquid confidence.

I felt victorious strutting back to Piper. Pimps walk with less swagger. She was overjoyed by my double-fisted makeover. She was even more grateful that I gave her the full beer, which I presented as a gentleman's offering and not the get-the-girl-drunk-so-she'll-kiss-you maneuver I intended. It was the first time I bought a girl a free drink, and it was paying off.

"Adam, I'm so glad I saw you here," she said.

"You are?"

"Yeah, I really like hanging out with you." Piper paused to take a sip. "And Shane."

His name entered my ears like a knife. I tried not to groan. Maybe she was just making a conciliatory remark about a member of the host committee. Whatever her reason, I had little time to stay wounded. An all too familiar sight reappeared by the front gate: The cop car was back.

This time it brought five more cars. Once, a man was killed at the local ice cream shop and only *four* cop cars arrived at the scene. This party carried more weight than murder.

While my junior nervous breakdown reemerged in full-force, the age-appropriate party guests cheered when they saw the police parked on the street below. Chants of "Lock the gate!" and "Fuck the cops!" failed to harmonize, but helped to lighten the mood. Several macho jock types even rose to the occasion and sprinted down the driveway to ensure the gate was locked.

I asked a couple by my side what happened if the gate was locked. They told me some spiel about private property, breaking and entering, how it was illegal—and then they casually offered Piper and I some marijuana. We both declined and continued drinking our beers while we studied what happened after the gate was locked. The cops remained in their cars and the partygoers marched through a tiny gap in the adjacent hedges and proceeded up the driveway.

There must've been a hundred people entering the mix, which would put the total attendance at around three hundred.

-8-

As the night moved toward midnight, there were more than five hundred people stuffed into Shane's mom's boyfriend's house. Crazed drunkards were cannonballing off the second story roof into the pool. Dancing drunkards were jumping on the furniture. Horny drunkards were fucking in the bushes. And teenage drunkards, like me, were in awe.

In the midst of the mayhem, I saw Uncle Russ holding a pile of landline telephones he collected from around the house. I guess his goal was to stop word-of-mouth from traveling farther than anyone could yell, but it was about as effective as using beach towels to slow a tidal wave. People kept pouring in through the leak in the hedges and I was happily submerged with Piper Purdy.

She and I were locked at the hip, flirting with our mouths hovering next to one another's. A solid jolt on either one of our backs would've catalyzed our first kiss and awarded me the prize that my chickenshit brain couldn't win on its own. Eventually, a jolt arrived, but it felt more like a tug and it pulled me in the opposite direction of Piper's mouth.

"Adam, where the hell is Shane?"

It was a very rattled Uncle Russ. He appeared less pleased about Shane's lengthy absence than me.

"I don't know, Uncle Russ. Why?"

"Well, because the cops are coming up the driveway."

I'm not sure what illegal maneuvers they took to get in, or if the lock was as crappy as the gate, but the police managed to break through our last line of defense. In minutes, a dozen officers would be arriving at the house, armed with handcuffs small enough to confine my bony wrists. Uncle Russ ordered me to find the rest of the slumber party and hide upstairs where the cops were unlikely to explore. It was a game-changing order. I still needed to lock lips with Dream Weaver, but I couldn't possibly execute an already ballsy maneuver with an older dude breathing down my neck.

"Piper, will you wait for me upstairs?"

"Yes!" she replied, as if to say she'd wait for me forever—or until she went to high school and started dating a badass senior and forgot my name.

I took off and began searching the house for middle-schoolers. Thankfully, I found Anton, Chris, Seth, Casey, and Edgar in the guest house smoking weed from a three-foot bong. None of them knew of Shane's whereabouts, and due to their lengthy pot intake, they were pretty clueless about their own whereabouts. They still understood that cops wouldn't condone their non-medicinal ritual, so they hustled upstairs.

As I continued my hunt for Shane, I located Joni Novack in the kitchen. She was not refining her loose sexual tendencies on my best friend, but she was making out with a pro surfer. I carried on, looking through several downstairs rooms for Shane, when it became apparent that I should probably be looking out for my own ass. Through a large window in the living room, I saw the police fleet rounding the last bend in the driveway and marching steadily toward the front door. They were equipped with all the murderous essentials plus a spot-lit video recorder. For all I knew, I was going to be a blurry-faced kid peeing his pants on an episode of *Cops*, so I backtracked to the pool and sought the protection of my veteran leader.

"Uncle Russ! I can't find Shane and the cops are coming in the house right now!"

Uncle Russ looked beyond me to the hundreds of maniacs that were pillaging his once peaceful luau. The party was no longer under his control. It was total anarchy. I watched several men nearly clip his head as they plum-meted into the pool; then Uncle Russ started walking away from me.

"Wait! Where are you going?"

"I'm getting the hell out of here!"

"Well, what the fuck should I do? I'm just a kid!"

He turned and said, "Don't get arrested, grommet," before he disappeared into the house and forfeited his overnight guardian title.

I was all alone. And then it hit me: I had sent Piper on a direct path to Shane. My best friend. My worst enemy. He was upstairs where I told him sexual favors were awaiting him.

If idiots got awards, I would've been presented a blue ribbon.

-9-

When I reached the upstairs living room, I saw a few adults hanging around, oblivious that the party was under siege by the entire police department. I darted past them like I was covered in flames and found Piper patiently wait-ing near the back patio. My greatest fear proved false; Shane didn't have his tongue in her mouth. In fact, he was

nowhere in sight. As I came within smooching distance of
Piper, I had trouble mobilizing my own tongue for a kiss,
or even a word. Rather than wait for me to rediscover the
English language, Piper suggested we hide from the cops
in the nearby guest bedroom.

The mood was set: a secluded, dark bedroom. If it were
any more cinematic, a Boyz II Men ballad would've been
playing in the background. Piper stepped close, alerting
me that it was time to make my move. So I readied my
quivering lips and leaned in for the greatest moment of
my life. Then something interrupted my destiny. A horri-
ble bodily symphony filled the room. It was a mean, bel-
lowing barf sound followed by a splash of liquid smack-
ing the floor. We both turned toward the noise and saw
someone emerge from under a futon in the corner of the
room. I turned on a light to get a clearer view. It was Shane,
covered in puke. He actually made it to the back bedroom
(the *waaaaay* back part) and must've been too loaded to
return to the party.

"Oh my God!" Piper cried, "Are you all right?"

"Yeah, he's fine. He does this all the time," I said, then
turned off the lights to restore order.

I couldn't let Shane's barfing put a damper in my
mission to kiss the girl. I also couldn't stop the cops from
coming upstairs. The blinding rays of flashlights appeared
on a concrete wall outside the bedroom and they were
growing wider with each millisecond. I could hear the
static from walkie-talkies turning into audible voices,
which meant the police were closing in on the moment I

was failing to seize. I had one last chance to drop my lips on Piper—and one last chance to save Shane from incarceration. As usual, I went where Shane went.

"Piper, there's a staircase on the other side of the bedroom that leads down to the driveway. The cops won't see you. Hurry!"

She idled a moment, waiting for the kiss that should've been on her lips, then she ran away. Right before the cops came upstairs, I grabbed Shane and scampered across the living room to his bedroom. The coast was clear. Almost. There were no locks on Shane's door. When police enter a property in groups of ten or more, I figured it was protocol to inspect what lies behind every unlocked door. Furthermore, there was a seamless window pane on one side of the bedroom, which meant any officer walking along the adjacent patio could see directly inside the room. The last place to hide was inside Shane's tiny bathroom. So I grabbed Shane by his barf-covered collar and yanked him into the room.

Due to moisture accumulation from Shane's long masturbation showers, the sliding wood door was completely warped. I pushed the swollen piece of hardwood with all my measly strength, but it was still wedged open a good ten inches—ample space for someone to look inside. With no safer option, Shane and I huddled behind the door as the cops patrolled outside his bedroom.

"Whatever you do, Shane, don't make a sound," I whispered.

He stared at me with fear hammering through his eyes.

"I'm sorry, Adam," he said and began barfing uncontrollably.

While bile spewed from his mouth, I moved Shane to the sink and noticed the bedroom door open through a reflection off the mirror. Two male officers, both slightly overweight and aged toward retirement, stepped inside. I looked back at Shane, hoping he saw them and that panic would disrupt his puking. His body continued to convulse, as if he were summoning vomit from the Earth's core. We were doomed. One of the cops caught an earful of the noise and stalked its path.

For the first time since I was a child, I wrapped my arms around Shane and cried. We grew up too fast in one night. I knew the real casualty of innocence lost would be our friendship, because I would forgive Shane for being a bad influence, but I didn't think my parents ever would. Luckily, fate was more forgiving than my mom or dad.

"Fuck off, pigs!" a boy shouted.

It wasn't Shane, though it took me a moment to determine if his vocal cords had read my mind. I watched the cops swing their flashlights toward the bedroom window and up the lush canyon. Fifty feet up the hill were Anton, Casey, Seth, Edgar, and Chris, their eyes shining through the grass like stoned hyenas. The officers rushed outside to confront our saviors.

"You're in big trouble, kids! Get down here, *now*!"

There was a long, contemplative pause before Chris responded.

"*No way!*"

The cops fumed while they hollered more threats up the hill. Finally, they turned to one another.

"Do you really wanna climb all the way up there and get these little bastards?"

"Hell, no! You know I've got knee problems."

"Yeah, I thought I was going to have a heart attack just walkin' up that damn driveway."

"Tell me about it."

"Should we split?"

"Yeah, I'm pretty hungry."

The cops retreated inside and out of view. I stood silent behind the door, sweating bullets the size of bombs, until my friends descended the hill. The police were gone, which meant my invaluable friendship with Shane would live to see at least one more adventure.

-10-

An hour later, after Shane finally stopped blowing chunks, we all convened in the ravaged living room to watch a surf movie and decompress from the most intense night of our lives. Uncle Russ eventually stumbled through the front door with some Domino's pizzas, adding a little more truth to the lies we had told our parents.

Before Shane dozed off into hangover dreamland, he asked me, "Did you finally make out with Piper?" I regretfully said no. It still pains me to think that I didn't get to kiss the girl of my dreams that night. But then again, neither did my best friend.

Me and Shane in seventh grade.

MEETING MAJESTA

-1-

"Is Bob there?"

It was a woman—a *young* woman. I was watching MTV in my bedroom when I answered the phone. My dad had just stepped out to buy some cigarettes.

"No, he's not here right now. Can I take a message?"

There was a long pause on the other end of the line.

"No, that's fine. I'll, uh, try back another time. Bye."

Like a typical twelve-year-old, I cared more about the video on the TV than the stranger on the telephone. I hung up and kept watching.

-2-

I was very young when I realized my dad was a badass. My old man, Bob Mars, rode motorcycles with a notorious gang of hot-blooded anarchists in the '60s. The motorcycle club was called the Gypsy Nomads and they were L.A.'s version of *A Clockwork Orange* on wheels.

Bob joined the club the day he bought his first Harley at age fifteen. Four years of life-threatening excess later, the gang was gone. After several violent encounters with their rival gang, a Hell's Angels sister club called the Satan's Slaves, the few surviving members of the Gypsy Nomads disappeared into the seedy underworld of southern California and never spoke again.

By the time I entered the world, my dad ditched the outlaw biker life for the slightly more civilized career of a kitchen chef, but the outlaw life never left him. He still drank, he still smoked, he still carried weapons, he still fought, he still got arrested, and the words LIVE TO RIDE, RIDE TO LIVE were still tattooed on his arm. While he didn't like to openly tell me about his checkered past, sometimes he would get drunk with his kitchen buddies and his past would peek its crazy head.

One time when I was seven, I remember my dad and his friends were hanging out in my parents' bedroom and they sounded like they were having more fun than me. Being a curious spoiled brat, I threw a big enough tantrum that my dad let me see what all the fuss was about. It wasn't the latest Atari game that was causing a commotion. It was a collection of illegal firearms—guns that could kill anyone, including the Terminator—that was making his buddies go nuts.

As I gawked at the metallic inspirations behind my own arsenal of toy guns, I noticed some old photographs of scary guys on motorcycles next to a sawed-off shotgun.

When I asked who the people in the photos were, my dad said they were his old friends. When I asked where they were now, he said they were dead.

-3-

Five years later, my family went on one of our many budget vacations to someplace that was less of a resort paradise than our hometown. This time we went to Pismo Beach, California—the Clam Capital of the World! Like many families in America, the Mars clan was trying to make the most of life in a lousy recession. My parents ran a respectable catering company, but money was always tight, and considering the amount of time they argued about bills, I was surprised we had enough money to take a trip outside of our own front yard.

After a few boring days in Pismo, I woke up to the sight of my dad putting on his nicest suit. He stood only five feet eight inches tall, but he commanded his space like a giant. His barrel chest and thick arms complemented his broad face, which would never be considered pretty, but handsome in most lighting. After my little brother, Alex, came into the picture, he trimmed his long brown hair and menacing mustache to acceptable professional lengths. And if you didn't know better, you'd think he was just another harmless blue-collar guy—not a rebel who could rip your head off.

Once my dad was dressed, I saw him whisper something to my mom. Her olive-toned skin lost most of its color when he walked out of the room.

"Mom, where's Dad going?" I asked.

"He's visiting one of his friends he grew up with," she said, then forced a smile.

Memories of the night my dad clued me in on his lack of youth-era pals came back to me in an instant. I thought about telling my mom what he had told me—that all his old friends were terminated—but I had outgrown my nosey-tattletale phase and entered my introverted-oldest-son phase. I didn't say anything.

-4-

Six months later, I answered our home phone. A familiar voice filled my ear.

"Hi, is Bob there?"

He was home. The whole family was huddled around the TV, watching *The Simpsons* and having the closest thing to a proper sit-down dinner we knew how to have. This time, there was a long pause on my side of the line. My parents were arguing a lot those days and my dad would sometimes leave angry and come home hours later. It was no secret that before Bob Mars retired his single status, he had a reputable career as a self-proclaimed gynecologist. Hundreds (maybe thousands) of women had sought out his sexual services, and I worried this lady might be part of an occupational relapse.

"Is it for me?" my dad asked.

I nodded and handed him the phone.

"Hi, this is Bob."

He froze when the woman greeted him back.

"Oh, good evening…No, it's all right. I'll go to my office where it's not so loud."

His tone was very professional, but there was noticeable tension in his jaw. He walked downstairs to his office and closed the door.

"Who was that on the phone?" my mother asked.

I wasn't ready to throw my dad under the bus for being a cheat. Besides, the lady could've been calling about a wedding, or a corporate dinner, or how to prepare seared goat.

"Someone asking about catering…I think."

I was only half lying. My mom bought it and we carried on with our half-assed family dinner.

-5-

Over the next few years, I encountered that voice several more times. When she called asking for Bob, I said that he wasn't home. He usually *was* home, but I didn't feel like being the middleman in my family's demise. Besides, if this dumb twat was stupid enough to call when Bob's wife and kids were home, why should I help her out? At fifteen years old, I could've executed an affair better than her.

More importantly, she was making me resent my dad. I never figured him for a dumb twat lover. Sure, my mom had trouble spelling most three-letter words, but she wasn't stupid. Maybe my dad was just looking for someone that didn't have the mental capacity to be a nag. My mom won a gold medal in the Nagging Olympics. She could also squash the competition in the Biggest Sweetheart category of any spousal contest and was not the kind of woman you traded for a younger downgrade.

Regardless, I was pretty sure my parents were going to get divorced. Though they never got physical, their arguments became so frequent that I assumed they'd just run out of things to bitch about and shake hands and go their separate ways. Besides, the only thing more common in Orange County than sunshine or boob jobs was divorce. I was already comfortable with the other two. Maybe I'd adapt to the third.

Every day, I'd come home from school expecting to hear the official divorce report. Then one summer afternoon, when thoughts of perfect beach days distracted me from my parental storm, I stopped by to grab my surfboard. As I walked upstairs, I overheard my dad talking. And then I heard the dumb twat. The living, breathing, home-wrecking monster behind the voice was in my house and I was unprepared for the ambush. It's not that easy to walk into a room and start screaming at your mother's replacement. It's a lot easier to walk away because you'd rather not experience your first ass-whooping at the hands of your own father. So I turned around and headed back down the stairs.

"Adam?" my dad shouted.

The creaking of the stairs must've tipped him off.

"Yeah?"

"Come upstairs, please."

What an asshole, I thought to myself.

"All right. I'll be right there," I said.

Time drew to a sloth-like crawl as I lurched up the stairs and looked into our living room. The dumb twat was seated on the sofa closest to me. She was younger than I expected. Prettier, too. She had long blonde hair with dark roots and she wore a checkered short dress that barely held down her sizable chest blimps. But what really caught my attention was her face. We had the *same* nose, and the *same* forehead, and the *same* eyebrows. When I saw that my mother was also in the room, smiling like I hadn't seen in months, I knew my previous assumptions about this alleged twat were a little off.

"Hi, I'm Majesta," she said.

My dad felt the need to solve the puzzle—as if I needed to buy a vowel.

"She's your sister."

-6-

The first time Bob and Majesta met, they sat across from one another in a restaurant near Pismo Beach. No amount of age or experience could've prepared the forty-two-year-old man and the fifteen-year-old girl for that day. Five years before, a heated argument between Majesta and her mother had pushed Majesta to say what she had always thought to be true—that the jerk she grew up knowing as her biological father was not her dad at all. Later that evening, Majesta was eavesdropping on her mother's phone call when she heard there might be some truth to the matter.

Majesta's mother, Sharon, had a wild relationship with Bob that ended before Majesta was born. Sharon left Bob for another man, and the possibility of a parental over-lap seemed unlikely. However, the erratic, drug-plagued nature of their split always kept Sharon wondering—espe-cially as Majesta's facial features came into form. Sharon still had ties to friends in Laguna, so one day she forward-ed a letter to Bob and a connection was established—a not-so-promising connection.

After Bob read the letter, he had one of their mutual friends head to Sharon's house in Morro Bay to do some detective work. Now, for whatever reason—whether Bob's amateur detective had poor vision or was just trying to protect him from a sticky situation—she said that Majesta didn't look anything like him and that there was nothing to worry about. Case closed...not quite.

Bob may have been a lot of bad things, but underneath his rebel façade, he was not a bad person. He was raised a bastard—the son of an abusive, unloving dickhead—and he knew all too well the pain that came from feeling like one didn't belong. So when another letter arrived in the mail—this time written by Majesta and containing her picture—Bob decided to meet this innocent-looking girl when he took his family on vacation.

Back at the restaurant in Pismo Beach, their conversa-tion began on a less innocent note.

"Will you go buy me a pack of cigarettes?" Majesta asked bluntly.

The chromosomes were really starting to match. Still, Bob never expected his first fatherly favor would involve contributing to the delinquency of a minor. It was easier than having a conversation, so he got up and went to the vending machine at the bar.

While he was gone, their waiter arrived. Majesta ordered a cheeseburger, medium rare with extra mayo. After Bob came back with the pack, they both lit up smokes and went mute. Awkwardness rose to record highs. Majesta put out her cigarette and excused herself to the restroom. Bob was robbed of his appetite. When the waiter returned, he ordered something to fill his side of the table. Sure, he could polish off a bologna sandwich in jail, no problem. But this meal was torture.

Eventually, Majesta came back and Bob started talking about nothing special. He approached the conversation like he was having drinks with a buddy. You know, something he was *good* at. Majesta, however, had been dreaming about this meeting for years. It was her one shot to solidify the bond that she so desperately desired and she wasn't going to wing it. Unfortunately, she had only heard about Bob Mars the outlaw, so her strategy to impress him involved lavish tales about the people she had beat up, the drugs she had taken, the crimes she had committed—and nothing about Barbies, ponies, or shopping. Bob was a good sport and rolled with the punches, but inside he was fucking terrified. Majesta was no angel. She was teenage

Bob Mars incarnate—his worst nightmare!

Their waiter arrived with food before Bob had heard enough. When the waiter relayed their orders, Bob and Majesta realized they ordered the same meal—right down to the extra mayo. Majesta raised her eyebrow like the little devil she was and Bob knew, then and there, there would be no need for a blood test.

-7-

"So," my mom asked, "is she your daughter?"

"She's mine. She's wild. And I don't know if I can bring her around our kids."

My dad called my mom after his meeting with Majesta rattled, to say the least. Parenting was already a difficult craft for Bob, but the introduction of an untamed teenager might destroy his entire family if he didn't handle her carefully. My mom was worried as well. Although she had always wanted to offset the empire of testosterone in our house with a daughter, she didn't think she'd have to bypass childbirth to get one. Her only experience with a family dynamic like this was through trashy daytime talk shows, and even then it looked frightening. The long-lost child's mother usually wanted payback for all the bills the father missed out on, and she would raise legal hell if he didn't pay up. Unfortunately, the Mars family finances were hovering right above flat broke, so this was going to be an interesting exchange.

With plenty on their minds, my parents returned home

and debated how they were actually going to graft this shaky new branch to our family tree. Meanwhile, *The Jerry Springer Show* would have to find talent elsewhere.

-8-

Majesta thought she might never hear from Bob again. Their parting after lunch was fine, but she knew that her bad girl performance didn't win her a new fan. The man she met and the father she envisioned were two different people. Had she not played up the scope of her wild streak for Bob's assumed amusement, maybe he would've welcomed Majesta into the Mars family with open arms. As it stood, Bob's arms were still crossed. And that's how things remained for several years.

During that time, Bob and Majesta would occasionally call one another, and my parents would send her gifts on her birthday and at Christmas. They even discussed meeting up again when she was free from school, but summers came and went. And my parents didn't want to be distant. They were just proceeding cautiously until Majesta's intentions became more clear. My mom even went so far as to see a psychic to find out what Majesta really wanted to gain from this relationship. She was relieved to hear that it was *love*. Majesta was just looking for love. And that was great, because my mom and dad had plenty of that. Child support or a new car would've been harder to come by.

-9-

"I want to go to Laguna and party with you and the girls."

That was Majesta's high school graduation request to her mother. She wanted to visit her two godmothers who lived in the beautiful beach town she had heard so much about. Seven days of sun and fun seemed like a fair reward for twelve grueling years of public school oppression. Yet, underneath her carefree party pitch, she really wanted to see Bob.

Majesta's stubborn pride helped move her primary goal to the back of her mind when she and her mother made the trip down south. But when sunburns and champagne hangovers lost their painful charm, Majesta's mind vacationed back to him. Somewhere in a town of several thousand strangers was her father. If she stayed around long enough, chances were they would run into one another. Sadly, her trip was running low on days and destiny didn't get the memo.

"You have to call him," Sharon said.

Majesta's mother knew the real motive for this adventure was ulterior all along. A single phone call could help Majesta and Bob reconnect, but it wasn't so simple. What if Bob didn't want to see her? It was a possibility—one that Majesta feared would put an end to their relationship altogether. She figured she was better off holding onto the scraps of something real than risking it all on something unknown. Her mother believed it was a risk worth taking, and after some hefty persuasion, Majesta put a muzzle on her fears and picked up the phone.

-10-

Mothers know best. The next evening, Majesta and Sharon met my parents at a lively sushi restaurant in town. Majesta had never eaten sushi before, so picking the same food wouldn't be the highlight of this meal. Nonetheless, Majesta quickly stole the show with a follow up performance that was no act at all. A few years of maturity had turned the auditioning rebel into a sweet (though not too sweet) young woman who was undeniably hilarious and impossible to dismiss. My mom loved her immediately. My dad was right there with her. Somehow, his reckless past had blessed him with a new partner in crime—one who wouldn't scare the shit out of him on a daily basis, but one that he would develop a caring relationship with from that day forth.

The following afternoon, my dad went against his previous reservations and introduced Majesta to my brother and me. She passed our inspection, moved in shortly after, and our family has never been the same. Thank God.

Majesta, me, and Alex. First family meeting.

THE VIRGIN EXPLORERS

-1-

I was born with the adventurous spirit of a timid sloth. My mother's side of the family had a rich history of staying too close to their nest. My Grandpa Mario hated traveling so much that it took a world war to get him to leave California. My Uncle Mike drove Ferraris, but he never rode an airplane because he thought they went too fast. My mother's fear of flying was only slightly less severe, and as a child she introduced me to educational films such as *La Bamba* and *The Buddy Holly Story*.

Mental scarring aside, I was content living as a hometown prisoner. I lived two blocks from the beach and summer was typically a ten-month season in southern California. Unfortunately, the Pacific Ocean didn't cooperate with extended heatwaves. The water around Laguna Beach was cold and stayed cold—sometimes all year. As a poorly insulated surfer, I found it challenging to maintain the ideal level of stoke during winter. Wise men didn't give condoms the nickname 'wetsuits' because they felt good.

By the spring of my high school sophomore year, I was really horny for some unprotected surfing. Tropical surf movies were no substitute for the real thing, and they were less satisfying than porn. But I couldn't come up with a vacation plan on my own. It had to be orchestrated by someone else, then I had to be cattle-prodded to go along.

One morning, as we thawed out from a chilly surf session, my good friend Walt Hagstrom suggested that we go to Puerto Vallarta to score some warm waves and hot babes for spring break. Walt was a blonde, blue-eyed surfer dude with an unbalanced wild side that led him to exotic lands far beyond our zip code. He told me that Puerto Vallarta was a tropical paradise filled with uncrowded waves, eighty-degree water, and tourist girls with poor morals. Travel phobias get nuked when a description like that invades the brain. My Mexico vacations never extended beyond Baja and my most notable memory of that country was being held at gunpoint by *federales*. I figured timid sloths might do better farther south, so I agreed to go along on the adventure, if it was cool with my parents.

-2-

Sending your sixteen-year-old child to a foreign country without a cell phone is unimaginable. Horror movies are developed around less scary concepts. But in 1997, it was the norm. My mom and dad ultimately green-lit my trip because Walt's parents were educated people and they believed we could survive five days abroad. Walt's mother handled the travel plans and rented us a nice condo in the heart of the city. She also gave us a list of local taxi companies, restaurants, and emergency services. Every move was mapped out. All we had to do was get to our destination.

To ease my travel anxiety, my mom supplied me with two pills of Ativan—one for the flight there, one for the flight back. By the time we reached the runway in our Delta airplane, I had already knocked back both pills and was happily drooling on myself. The weather didn't pose any threat—partly cloudy with light winds—but I knew I could get super drunk before flying home and achieve comparable results.

Ten minutes after takeoff, my soaring adrenaline turned the Ativans into placebo pills. Every minor shake made my knuckles a lighter shade of white as I tried to steer the plane with my seat dividers. Meanwhile, Walt calmly flipped through a *Surfer* magazine and tried to start a conversation.

"Stop being such a bitch, Adam. We're fine."

"But why is the plane making that noise?"

"Because it's a plane, *not* a bicycle."

He was right, but I kept panicking and continued steering the plane.

"Dude, seriously take a chill pill," he joked.

"I did! I took two!"

"What?" he yelled. "Gimme one, asshole!"

When I told him my supply ran out, he did his best to heighten my anxiety the rest of our three-hour flight with ridiculous tales of plane rides gone wrong. As we began our descent, I finally managed to block out Walt's rant. Not because he stopped yapping, but a deafening pressure built up in my head, leaving me deaf and woozy. One of the after-effects of surfing in polluted water was that my ears were constantly infected, but I didn't know how badly until I dropped 30,000 feet out of the sky. In desperate need of relief, I labored through all the common cures: chewing gum, pinching nose, banging head against window. Nothing worked.

When we screeched onto the tarmac, I was sure my eardrums would burst open and I'd be in serious trouble. Walt even looked concerned. He knew I wasn't being a bitch for dramatic purposes.

"Please don't let me die on an airplane," I begged.

"The plane already landed. You're not gonna die. Just wait until they depressurize the cabin. That should fix it."

On cue, the pilot said he just depressurized the cabin. Strangely, my inner ear didn't believe him and refused to make the necessary adjustments. The pressure was excruciating, pounding against every cell in my head with the force of a trillion taquitos. But there was no turning back. I literally asked the pilot if he would fly me home, and he said no.

-3-

I lurched through the terminal dragging my heavy surf-board bag like Quasimodo on vacation. Older, weaker tourists passed me with ease as I tried to keep pace with Walt. He seemed confident navigating the chaotic airport, and despite feeling downright awful, I felt I was in good hands. Before we reached the taxi station, Walt stopped short. His eyes locked onto a prize.

"I'm gonna rent a car."

"Why? I thought your mom said we could take cabs everywhere."

"Dude, this will be *way* better."

I no longer felt I was in good hands. Walt was a maniac behind the wheel—an accomplished maniac that had already accumulated as many speeding tickets as the law would allow. In Mexico, where drivers were more aggressive, there was no telling what level of recklessness he would strive for. But I had a safeguard. He wasn't old enough to rent a car.

"Don't you have to be in your twenties to rent one?" I asked, aware that I was 100% correct.

He thought a moment, trying to recall the Rental Car Constitution, then said to me with a smirk, "Maybe."

Yeah, right! No fucking way was Walt going to rent a car. He was sixteen. A toddler had a better shot at buying cigarettes. But I didn't bother arguing. Someone would surely be laughing in his face in a few moments, then we could get into a taxi as planned.

Walt led me past Hertz, Avis, Budget, and other reputable companies before settling on a local brand with the most meager display of the pack. A red vinyl banner with MexiCar written in yellow block letters hung above a small office station. Behind the counter, a young woman with heavy, clown-like makeup punched numbers into an outdated desktop computer. There was no one in line, which should've been the first (or fourth) red flag, but Walt approached the counter unfazed.

"Hello! Welcome to Puerto Vallarta!" she said in perfect English.

"*Howla, senyoreeetuh. Yow key-yerrow oooh-nnn coh-chay, por fayver.*"

Walt had a distinct surfer-bro accent that muddied Spanish into a new language that only gringos could understand.

"Excuse me. Are you trying to rent a car?" she asked.

Walt made a universally known gesture and nodded.

"Great! Would you like a large car or a small car?"

"Um, I would like a *cheap* car."

I unintentionally nodded along, knowing we were farther away from baller status than California.

"Well, we have a Volkswagen Beetle. Do you know how to drive stick?"

Walt said yes, and she began prepping the contract. I couldn't believe his plan was going along so smoothly. Then his plan hit a pothole.

"I just need your license."

Walt stayed calm. He recently transferred from a preppy private school to a bully-run public school without getting his ass kicked. He wasn't intimidated by a gentle desk clerk. Walt handed over his license and waited. She studied the card, then broke the news with a sad face.

"I'm sorry, Mr. Tapp, but you're only twenty-one. You have to be at least twenty-five to rent a car in Mexico."

Mr. Tapp? *Twenty-one*? That sly fool slipped her his fake ID—a fake ID so bad that his name, Walter Hagstrom, was listed as some imaginary redneck superhero named Natter Tapp and his eye color was blonde. No joke. Eye color: BLN.

In a last-ditch effort, Walt erected a presidential smile and joked, "But I'm a really good driver!" He held his expression until wrinkles took shape. Shockingly, the woman began to cave. She looked over her shoulder for a superior. When one wasn't spotted, she turned to Walt and whispered, "Well, if you're *really* good, I guess it's okay."

My brain almost blew a fuse. For twenty bucks a day, we got our own car. The clerk typed Natter Tapp's information into her computer, then mentioned some costly details.

"Now, since you're so young, I can't give you any insurance. You just have to take extra-special care of the car, or else you'll have to pay for all the damages and cleaning fees. Okay?"

She should've robbed us right there. I was in too much pain to argue with Walt, and he was in too deep to pull out. He handed over his dad's MasterCard, which didn't get a second glance from the desk clerk. She placed it in a manual imprint card machine, slid the handle across, handed him the receipt, and Walt forged his dad's signature. There were no mobile banking apps back then, so if our vehicle got totaled, Mr. Hagstrom wouldn't know that he purchased a dead Volkswagen until he got his monthly statement in the mail.

-4-

It was a Herbie: a white 1967 Volkswagen Beetle that had been reincarnated as the same vehicle. Apparently, Volkswagen never discontinued the production of their classic model in Mexico and rewarded America with uglier upgrades. A weathered man in his late fifties walked us around the vehicle, noting flaws and then marking them on a form. Even though the car was in almost pristine condition, we made sure his waning vision didn't overlook any costly dents.

After initialing the form, Walt received the keys. On the keychain was a nifty little security device, like a zip drive, which had to be inserted into a slot on the dashboard for the starter to engage. Hotwiring was also never discontinued in Mexico and the device was our only defense against thieves. Lastly, the generous man tied our surfboards onto the roof, then pointed us toward the exit. It was mid-afternoon and the hot air cooked my headache to unpleasant perfection. I couldn't wait to get to our condo and pass out next to the air conditioner. Dogs have more ambitious plans on vacation. But I hoped with a little rest, I could refocus on more important things like losing my virginity to a complete stranger.

I buckled up as Walt inserted the security device. He fired up the engine, gave the man a parting wave, and then stalled as he shifted into first gear. He went through this process three more embarrassing times before finally gaining momentum and zipping onto the main road.

"Walt, I thought you knew how to drive stick!"

"Dude, don't worry. I've driven my dad's car at least five times."

"*Five times*?" I yelled as I strangled my seatbelt.

"Hey, you can drive if you'd like."

I looked at the people around us, swerving between lanes and risking life to gain a few inches of pavement. It was Mexican *Mario Kart* with no pause button. On top of that, I didn't have a license and had trouble operating an automatic transmission. I declined Walt's offer.

-5-

We idled at the bottom of a steep street in a sketchy residential neighborhood a couple miles outside the heart of Puerto Vallarta—closer to its butthole. According to Mrs. Hagstrom's directions, our condo was located somewhere at the top of the hill.

"Maybe I made a wrong turn back in town."

"Hopefully," I said, mostly to myself.

Walt left on foot to get a better look. A few minutes later, he came down the mini mountain, gasping for air.

"Well...*this* is...the...place."

"Seriously?"

"Yup...it's not...so bad once...you get up there."

He lied. It was worse. The luxurious one-bedroom

condo featured twin beds with musty sheets, windows
without any screens, several windows without any glass,
a tiny black and white TV, a bathroom with half a roll of
toilet paper, a broken ceiling fan, and of course, no air conditioner.

"How the hell did your mom find this dump?"

"On the internet. I saw the pictures. It looked nice."

The photos must've been taken the day it was built in
the '60s. Walt and I bickered about how we were going to
survive in our glorified tent before he stormed out to buy
beer. Once I was alone, my headache completely consumed me. I needed relief. But how? When you're sixteen,
you dream about being thousands of miles away from your
parents. You never consider that it means you're the same
distance away from your personal physician. So I had to
pinpoint the cause of my discomfort. Something—earwax
or poison gas—was blocking my ear passages. If I could
remove it, the pressure would deflate and I would feel
normal again.

I began my recovery process by slamming my head into
the least smelly bed a few dozen times. The bed springs
killed some precious brain cells, but did nothing to relieve
the pressure. Next, I raised the bar with an invasive device.
Using the pointy end of my toothbrush, I penetrated my
left earhole and tried to unclog the pipe. Immediately, I
scratched the inside of my canal and collapsed onto the
bathroom floor in tears. There, at my most vulnerable, I
saw a plunger. A long wooden handle with a red rubber
cap balanced proudly beside the toilet. How many close

encounters with Montezuma's Revenge did this shit-sucker have? More than one? More than *a million*? It didn't matter. I was beyond desperate. I placed the plunger up to my other ear, then I lunged the handle inward. The flat rim engaged with my face—indicating that I had optimum suction. I pulled back swiftly and *abracadabra*! Nothing happened but a fart sound.

I collapsed against the wall, defeated. Amidst a new batch of tears, I saw a tiny green lizard scamper across the floor and over the plunger. He didn't even stop to give me a look. He had seen people in worse condition in that bathroom before.

-6-

Two agonizing days later, I recovered. It didn't take a doctor's expertise or Liquid Drano, but somehow I awoke to perfect ear pressure. Walt seemed even more relieved. My painful condition left me allergic to any type of fun and I knew I was ruining his trip. But with my body restored, I wanted to make up for lost time. The waves went completely flat in town, so we ditched our surfing plans and prepared to get laid.

Neither of us were hotties. We had potential, but we were stuck in that awkward phase where our features didn't fit properly on our bodies. Walt's six-foot-two frame and dangly arms were too big for his small head and pointy little ears. I maxed out at five-six and wore a floppy sun-bleached afro to cover my oversized forehead, which was more like a fivehead or a sixhead. Still, we estimated that with the right accessories, we could attract some desperate skanks. So we wore our nicest button-down shirts and Dockers khakis, threw some styling wax in our hair, and doused ourselves in enough Aqua di Gio to clear out a nightclub.

At ten o'clock, Walt and I took a taxi to the popular social establishments in town. Walking down the crowded cobblestone roads, we imagined we were Trent and Mikey entering the casino in the movie *Swingers*, dressed to kill and cocky as hell. Coincidentally, as in the movie, our environment teemed with elderly tourists. Not a teenage girl in sight. It quickly dawned on me that no parents were crazy enough to unleash their high school daughters in Puerto Vallarta for spring break.

"Walt, I thought you said there were tons of girls here last year!"

"There were, dude! Maybe they're inside the clubs."

Slim chance, but we had to find out. Walt and I passed clubs with colored lights and terrible Top 40 hits. From outside they looked dead—mostly local men mulling about to the sounds of Ace of Base and Hootie & the Blowfish. Farther down the street, a crowd of youthful tourists congregated outside a swanky building flanked by palm trees. We entered the line, trying to gauge the club's entrance policy. I didn't have a real *or* a fake driver's license, so I needed to appear at least eighteen. I unbuttoned my shirt to expose my two chest hairs and gave my most macho scowl as we neared the bouncers. Walt got in no problem as Natter

Tapp, but I got stopped.

"ID!" said a ripped guy in a black suit.

"I, uh, lost it last night," I replied in a deep, phony rasp like I had terminal laryngitis, "but I am eighteen."

"Sorry, amigo. No ID, can't come in."

He nudged me aside. Over his shoulder, Walt made desperate hand gestures implying that I should offer a bribe.

"Can I get in if I give you five bucks?"

"No ID... *fifty* bucks."

At that price, I would've had to survive on lizard meat the rest of the trip. I signaled to Walt that I wasn't coming inside. He made even more desperate hand gestures, which I interpreted as, "I hate you! I'm gonna kick your ass! You're the worst travel partner *ever!*"

The bouncer settled for twenty dollars, and once we got inside, Walt and I discovered plenty of women, but no girls. They danced in tight packs, drinking cocktails from oversized glasses with neon straws the size of churros. Some looked like college students. Others looked like they were expediting divorce. As high school people, Walt and I usually hooked up with girls our own age or younger. Rarely did we have physical encounters with someone a grade above us. Three to thirty years older? Forget about it. But those were the statistics we had to work with, so we found a table on the outside patio and brainstormed how to attract older females. First, we started chain-smoking Marlboro Reds to speed up the aging process. Then we ordered 32-ounce bottles of Pacífico to rival the ladies' mega-beverages. Nothing says sexy like 'I stink of tobacco and too much beer,' but our virgin minds believed we would improve our chances if we stuck with that formula.

An hour later, neither one of us got more than an accidental glance from the opposite sex. Then two women set up camp near our table: a redhead and a brunette in their early twenties, both freakishly sunburned and draped in loose blouses. They were too unpolished to be hookers. However, they weren't hideous, and Walt figured they were a good match for guys with no game.

"Hey, we should go talk to those ones," he suggested.

"Definitely."

Neither one of us moved a muscle.

"When?" I asked.

"I don't know, dude. Maybe *now*?"

"Okay."

We guzzled the rest of our beers and rose to the occasion.

"So, we're really going over there, Walt?"

"Yeah. Aren't we?"

"Totally. I just wanted to make sure."

"Cool. Let's go, dude."

A long, uncomfortable pause.

"How about let's order one more beer."

"Good call!"

"We don't want to be too aggressive," I said, then watched two aggressive local guys swoop in and steal the women.

Walt and I continued our cowardly pursuits the rest of

the night while we drank beer and smoked cigarettes until we ran out of money. We staggered home after midnight using each other to keep from falling over. Our friendship began under similar conditions. At a party earlier in the school year, I got stuck in a bush while I was running from the cops and was too hammered to pull myself out. Walt didn't know me very well, but he lent a helping hand and made sure I got home safely. The following weekend, Walt played the role of least desirable drunk at a festivity near my house. When no one offered to babysit the new kid, I paid him back by letting him puke his brains out in my bathroom and crash on my floor. Since then, our buddy system evolved, enabling us to get completely shit-faced at the same time.

Walt and I reached our neighborhood unharmed, though we couldn't manage our vertical street on foot and had to crawl to our condo, laughing at one another while curious neighbors monitored our progress. When we finally reached the front door, Walt stood tall and declared, "We may not have scored any chicks tonight, Adam, but tomorrow we're gonna surf good waves, or die trying!"

I laughed all the way inside. I thought he was joking.

-7-

We strapped our surfboards onto the Herbie and headed north at noon. Consumed by hangovers, we failed to leave at dawn when the conditions were best. Strong winds ripped through town, blistering the ocean with thick whitecaps. Thankfully, Walt knew of a place an hour away called Punta Burro where the sea might be better protected. Leaving Puerto Vallarta, the four-lane highway became a two-lane racing strip that weaved through miles of dense jungle. Pedestrian vehicles jockeyed with shipping trucks around every turn, passing into oncoming traffic like professional daredevils. Walt loved that road. He may have sucked shifting into first gear, but he was a natural blazing through fourth.

As we zipped along at max speed, I tried to distract my anxiety by staring at the beautiful scenery. Amidst the maze of greenery, I noticed a number of colorful signs alongside the road. They could've been distance indicators, but they appeared far too frequently. As Walt decelerated around a huge turn, I got a better view of one. It was a painted cross draped in dead flowers. A minute later, I saw another. Thirty-seconds after that, *another*. Over the course of a kilometer, I spotted seven. We were driving on a paved cemetery.

It would've been a shame to get killed in such an average car, so I begged Walt to slow down. He eased off the gas and eventually we emerged from the jungle with a different view of the Pacific Ocean. The sea was calm and swell lines pumped toward the coastline. We both hooted in celebration. We were going to surf after all.

Twenty minutes later, Walt pulled off at an empty bluff overlooking the sea. Below the rocky cliff, a dirt path zigzagged down to a cove where beautiful waves flowed in, unridden. We quickly unpacked our boards and ran down to the beach. The rich blue ocean felt better than bathwater against my skin as I paddled out on my new six-foot shortboard. While our friends were back home fighting with local assholes over ankle-high chop, Walt and I rode perfect head-high peaks without another surfer trying to steal our fun. It was truly an *Endless Summer* experience in spring.

After a few hours, our adrenal glands were drained and our limbs were about to fall off. Walt and I strolled back to the car, already planning our next ten surf trips. We figured after traveling the world, we'd become high-paid professional surfers with more groupies than Kelly Slater. Delusions aside, my whole perspective on travel changed that afternoon and I realized I was really an adventurer cloaked in chicken shit. Finally, the chicken shit washed away.

Walt and I got in the car, beaming, ready to kick off our last night in Mexico. He put the security device into the dash, turned the key, but the engine didn't start. Confused, he gave the device a good shake. A drop of clear liquid splattered onto the floorboard.

"What the heck is that, Walt?"

His mouth turned to marble. I had to chisel the answer out of him.

"It's saltwater," he said.

The idiot took the keys surfing! Somehow, he forgot that cheap electronic devices couldn't breathe underwater. Many failed insertions later, we stood above a small dip in the bluff.

"Now, when I yell *push*, you push the car and I'll jump

in and pop the clutch."

Walt yelled "*Push!*" and I leaned into the back panel. He hopped inside as the Herbie rolled down the dip. He screamed, "*Fuck!*" when the car came to a stop. We were stuck. Getting back to civilization would require another vehicle. Once again, I was a chicken shit posing as an adventurer.

Walt thought he could MacGyver the car back to life by messing with the engine. I opted for a more direct method and took to the highway. The next vehicle heading south would be crucial to our survival because I found myself standing in the middle of the road, waving my arms for help. An old white commuter bus motored toward me. It could've turned me into roadkill easier than it could've stopped, but it pulled off the road. I ran over to the driver—a thin Mexican guy with a gold front tooth—and put my four years of Spanish education to good use.

"*Perdón, señor, perro tenemos un problema con nuestra coche y necesitamos ir al aeropuerto. ¿Vas a Puerta Vallarta?*"

"*Si, señor. Cuesta tres pesos por persona.*"

"*¡Bueno!*"

I yelled toward Walt, "Hey, we got a ride! Grab your wallet and hurry the hell up!"

The bus was filled with fishermen returning home after a long day at sea. They wore ragged clothes stained by the blood of sea creatures and stunk of foul tuna. However, the two salty white boys stood out like fish flopping around a ship deck. We took a seat and didn't move the entire ride into town, hoping the fisherman wouldn't filet us if we looked unappetizing.

-8-

The stiff silent treatment worked and we reached the airport without incident. Heading to the MexiCar stand, Walt and I decided that playing dumb would be the best way to explain our broken security device. Fortunately, all of the incriminating saltwater dried up, so they gave us a new device and arranged for a ride back to our car—free of charge.

Two of MexiCar's top employees offered to chaperone. Decorated in violent scars and gang tattoos, they appeared to be waiting for two soldiers in the local cartel to die so they could take their jobs. In the meantime, they worked as rental car repairmen.

We drove away in the back of their lowered convertible Beetle. It was red. Again, that should've been *another* red flag, but we went along for the ride. Racing through the jungle, Walt and I got a better understanding of how people joined the roadside cemetery. Our driver spent little time in the proper lane. When he did, he tailgated and honked at cars already going over the speed limit. Walt could barely stomach the taste of his own medicine. He drove like a geriatric in a golf cart compared to this fucking madman.

Somehow, we survived the jungle without adding to the sum total of crosses. The final stretch of road covered mostly straight highway, which helped calm the fear magnifying in the back seat. Our driver stuck to his lane, though not for safety reasons. His copilot was serving him cocaine in a glass contraption called a bullet and he didn't want to spill any nose candy. Once the drugs kicked in, he started fender-fucking the Chevy Suburban in front of us. When he tried to pass, a Mack truck coming head-on blasted its horn. Our driver could've safely slipped back behind the Chevy, but he charged ahead. I went to fasten my seatbelt. There was no seatbelt. My only air bags were my lungs. Walt and I locked arms, bracing for impact. The Mack truck muscled forward. So did we. We were about to be mashed into extra-chunky salsa. Then, just before flesh merged with metal, our driver jerked the wheel and sent us off the road into a shallow ditch. We all screamed—well, Walt and I screamed. Our chaperones laughed their asses off. When the motor went dead, they got very angry and started arguing at Mach speed. Finally, the copilot opened up the trunk, where black smoke grew out of the engine. He mumbled something about a fluid leak, then he took off running back toward Puerto Vallarta, away from the finish line.

-9-

Sunsets are less pleasant when you're in the company of a coked-out creep. As the sky morphed into an inedible sorbet medley, our driver dished out bland tales about all the American girls he allegedly banged. All young, all beautiful, all rich. He had a venomous look that might attract girls with extreme daddy issues, though likely not. Walt and I mixed in the occasional, "That's awesome, dude" just to be safe. We didn't know how much longer we'd be stuck with Don Juan the repairman. His copilot had been gone a long time and whenever we asked when he'd be coming back, he said "Soon."

Soon turned into hours. Dinner time, to be more specific. If we would've taken taxis, we would've been scarfing tacos and celebrating our last night on vacation with more sexual rejections. But Walt wanted a rental car. At least now I wasn't solely responsible for ruining the trip.

Around nine o'clock, the copilot finally returned in the back of a rusty pickup. He jumped out carrying a plastic liter of some mechanical fluid. It cured the engine and we continued on to the bluff. There, we found our Herbie hiding in the dark. It was safe from thieves. It just wasn't safe from us. The new security device worked perfectly and our chaperones hustled us for ten bucks, then sped off toward the cemetery.

We gave them an extra-wide berth before getting back on the road. While we drove somewhat slowly into the jungle, I asked Walt what he wanted to do when we got back to town. Without taking a breath he said, "Pack." The leader of our expedition had been pushed beyond the boundaries of his wild side. So had I. Too many times in one day to count. I couldn't wait to get back to wetsuits and girls my age who wouldn't go all the way.

-10-

Although we had a full day to explore new surf spots, we couldn't risk another incident. So we put ourselves on house arrest until we needed to get to the airport for our 7:30 p.m. flight. By late afternoon, everything was in order. We made sure our condo looked as shitty as when we arrived. Finally, I got in the car and conjured some pre-flight paranoia while Walt tied down our surfboards. As he finished up, I saw him lean against his door for extra leverage. A strange popping sound followed.

"Son of a bitch!" he yelled.

"What happened?"

"Dude, I just dented the shit out of the door with my knee!"

I ran around the vehicle. A crater two-feet wide completely disfigured the door.

"Holy crap!" I said.

"They're gonna charge me a fortune, Adam! My dad's gonna kill me!"

I wondered why this possibility didn't factor into Walt's decision making when he signed his life over to MexiCar. Walt's dad was an imposing giant with hands that could choke an elephant.

"Walt, I bet someone can pop it out."

"Dude, we don't have time to get it repaired," he buried his head in his hands. "I'm dead!"

The car managed to ruin our day without even leaving the driveway. Now, Walt's life was in jeopardy. More likely his *social* life, but to a high schooler that's a death sentence. I gave Walt a supportive pat on the shoulder. Just then, I thought of a possible solution. A lizard raced across the side of the car. The same size, color, and breed I saw when we first arrived. I remembered watching him run across the bathroom floor—across the *plunger*.

-11-

We held onto the wooden handle and pushed into the car door with all our might. Not since average fools tried to pull Excalibur from stone had something been grasped with such force. As we yanked back, the plunger detached from the vehicle, sending us crashing to the ground. Dirtied and scuffed, we rushed over to inspect the dent. It vanished like a pimple in an infomercial. Walt and I hugged and howled with brutish joy, but one feature put an end to our happy ending. The pimple left a scar. A thin metal crease traced the boarder of the former crater. Visible to the eye and noticeable to the touch, the blemish kept Walt's life in limbo.

"Maybe they'll just charge you a percentage. I mean, the door's only about two percent ruined if you consider the total surface area."

That was the kind of stupid thinking that advanced math inspired. Walt hadn't passed algebra and understood the little ripple added up to a new door panel plus whatever ludicrous fee they wanted to tack on for installation.

"Fuck it," he said. "I was already gonna have to pay the

stupid cleaning fee. Let's just get the car really dirty and maybe they won't see the dent."

-12-

We found an empty lot where Walt spun the car in a dizzying pattern of donuts until we almost barfed all over the interior. Thankfully, we didn't maximize the cleaning fee, but still wound up with a good coat of dirt on the outside. Heading to the rental car parking lot, we still weren't sure if the dent would go unnoticed. Most adults were former conniving teenagers and could see right through a crooked plan. If our psycho chaperones surveyed the vehicle, we didn't stand much of a chance. We prayed that they finally got promoted to a prominent cocaine cartel, but when we pulled into the parking lot, they were still very much employed by MexiCar. The guys were inspecting a midsized sedan with meticulous detail and motioned for us to pull up behind.

"Dude, this isn't gonna work," Walt whimpered.

"Dude, I know."

"*Dude*! Don't say that!"

"*Dude*! *I'm just agreeing with you*!"

"*Dude, shut up*!"

Before we started strangling each other, the copilot appeared at Walt's window.

"¡*Hay, cabrón*! What happened to your car?"

"Well, sir, you see, there was lots of dust by our condo, but I really apologize for getting the vehicle dirty."

Walt's delivery was too artificially sweet to sound truthful. The copilot glanced at the hood, the roof, the rear. Meanwhile, the dent was eye-to-eye with his genitals. One look down and we were figuratively fucked.

"You know we're gonna have to charge you to clean the car, right?"

"Yeah, that's fine, sir. How much does that cost?"

"Hmm. We might have to wash it twice."

"*Two* car washes for *one* car?"

"*Si, señor*. Probably like forty bucks."

It was an obvious ripoff. But it was monetary music to our ears. Walt quickly fished the cash out of his wallet.

"*Un momento*. Lemme me see what Ricardo thinks." The copilot stepped back and hollered, "*¡Ricardo, ven aquí!*"

"No, it's okay, sir. We'll pay!" Walt reached for more cash. "How about forty-five! Or fifty!"

He didn't take the money. The one thing we couldn't afford was a fresh pair of eyes on the car. Yet, for some reason, when Ricardo was called, he didn't come over. Meanwhile, a blessing sauntered our way. The older man who first gave us our rental car walked out of a nearby garage hangar. He was *the real* Ricardo, and his eyes lacked any freshness.

For a discounted rate of only twenty dollars, Ricardo relieved Walt of his contract with MexiCar and wished us a safe flight. We still had thirty bucks and twenty minutes to kill, so we walked to a nearby liquor store and celebrated with a twelve pack. Walt and I sat under a long canopy drinking cold bottles of Corona in rapid succession. A light afternoon breeze pushed the pleasant aroma of gasoline from the runway to our noses, giving us a little extra buzz. When I got down to my last beer, I was less afraid to get on an airplane than ever before—not completely cured of my phobia, but I had a fresh selection of mental scars to keep me busy. At least Delta didn't make a convertible.

Walt and I searching for waves somewhere in Mexico.

YOU CAN'T SPELL COACHELLA WITHOUT HELL

-1-

The cops didn't know what to do with us. I sat in the back of a squad car with my college friends, Justin and Rachel. We were tired, cold, and caked in a heavy coat of desert filth. We were also coming down on a speedy batch of ecstasy and trying our hardest not to grind our teeth to pebbles when the officer glanced back at us. Not that it would've mattered. We had already been through an unfair amount of misfortune in the past seventeen hours, with plenty more awaiting us. We weren't going to be penalized further for trying to improve our moods with illegal substances.

Soon, the car came to a stop. The officer glanced back once more. We were nervous, but he warned us not to be shy. Naturally, the words flew from our mouths with amphetamine ease. He made no objections, then leaned out the window and relayed our requests.

"Yeah, I'd like three Sourdough Jacks, two large curly fries, some jalapeño poppers, a medium Diet Coke, and two extra-large Oreo Cookie shakes."

Suddenly, the "serve" in "serve and protect" drew new-found meaning as we idled in the fast food drive-through. Taxpayer money was going to good use—I promise. Along with nearly a dozen of my closest college friends, who were commuting in various police vehicles, I had gone to the Coachella Valley Music and Arts Festival with the best intentions. By now, we should've been back in our battered college rooms. Instead, we were lost in Palm Desert, we were starving, and as I mentioned earlier, we were in for more misfortune. Lots more.

-2-

It was April 2001, and Coachella was far from the universally known mega-concert that it has become. In its second official year, the event had been reduced to just a single day, and motivating large numbers of college kids to the blazing hot desert for a day of music, drugs, and dehydration was way more difficult than it is now.

I was a sophomore at UC Santa Barbara and I lived with a group of guys who shared my passion for music, partying, and partying. We were friends with all the best bands in town, we knew all the best drug dealers, and we were well on our way to turning our valuable academic year into a wonderful failure.

By the time discussions about a concert near Palm Springs began to circulate around our house, we were already dreading the fact that some of us would have to be sober drivers. It was a solid four-hour drive from UCSB to Coachella, and not a comfortable distance to navigate while on drugs.

As more friends became interested in the event and less friends offered to drive, it looked like our chances of making the voyage were slipping away. Then, like fate in the form of a fancy .jpg, a solution popped up on the Coachella website. It was a slick cartoon bus with the name Really Rockin' Busses scrolled out in bold font. For an additional sixty bucks, Really Rockin' Buses would drive anybody from Santa Barbara to the concert venue and back. To a bunch of guys who excelled in damaging their brains, it seemed like a no-brainer. Furthermore, the bus company's website was filled with moving graphics. In those days, websites weren't all hi-def displays of flash and style. Any website with clean graphics and no glitches was trusted as the sign of a quality company. Why people were so naive about web design, I don't know. We just *were.*

-3-

A school bus pulled up, mustard yellow and reeking of low-grade gas. It wasn't a newer box-shaped model, but a narrow, curved panel vehicle that I might have literally ridden in kindergarten. Despite the meager accommodations, our spirits were very high. We had assembled an epic gang of concertgoers from our posse of delinquent friends, and after all, transportation was simply the means to a better end. Even Napoleon crossed the Alps on a mule.

Now, if my memory serves me correctly, the people who made the Really Rockin' voyage were Shane, Blair, Emma, Michael, Corey, Rachel, Justin, Max, and Ronnie. Shane, Justin, Michael, Ronnie, and I all lived together in our own *Animal House*-style home, sans the douchebag fraternity element. The other names were friends that may as well have lived with us, but they paid rent elsewhere.

We all waited at the official boarding location near the Santa Barbara Municipal Airport with twenty other college and high school students who were also clients of Really Rockin' Buses. By mid-morning, it was cool and sunny, but desert temperatures were expected to reach the low hundreds, so we dressed accordingly. The girls opted for crop-tops and Daisy Dukes. The guys sported t-shirts and shorts. Most people brought backpacks filled with something warmer to wear on the way back. Some people, like Max, decided to pack their bag with a hundred pills of ecstasy. Those pills were meant to enhance our promising adventure and help a large number of people trip balls at the show. Max stood to make a lot of money from those pills. But like most things on that trip, they would cost us.

Before we loaded the bus, the old yellow door screeched opened. A dark-haired white male with a porn star mustache sat behind the wheel. He was to be the captain of our shitty ship. I never got his name. Then appeared the CEO of Really Rockin' Buses. He stood nearly six feet tall, weighed about two hundred and fifty pounds, and had a round face that would make a circle jealous. As he waddled down the steps, dressed in long cargo shorts and an XXL t-shirt with the same bus graphic from the website branded across his fat chest, we sensed that something was odd about him—aside from his attire. He looked a bit too young to be the owner of a car, let alone a company.

When a couple of haggard females in their late twenties followed him off the bus, flaunting the same shirts and holding official itineraries, our concerns began to dwindle. Their subservient mannerisms made it clear that he was in charge as he began to hand out company passes and break down our plans for the day. Our concerns perked up again when he told everyone to refer to him as Santa, but then again, plenty of people have crappy nicknames.

-4-

The journey to the desert was painless. We putted along in the yellow bus, roaming between rows and getting pumped up for the concert. Some of us gravitated to the back of the bus where the female crew stood guard over the complimentary snacks. The ladies of Really Rockin' Buses felt it necessary to flaunt their advanced ages over us college kids and were quick to belittle our supposed musical treats for the day. I had two musical goals: see Iggy Pop and see Jane's Addiction. Once I made that clear, they cut me some slack. My hip-hop fanatic friends, like Justin and Michael, failed to earn much praise from the rocker gals, so they moved up front. I decided to hang back and wax intellectual about my musical influences. Soon we were off topic and I couldn't help but ask about Santa.

"So, what's the deal with this Santa guy?"

"Oh, he's just a family friend."

"Yeah, he offered to pay for our tickets if we'd help organize the group, so we were like, fuck, yeah!"

"Cool. Well, I was just wondering because he looks super young," I said.

My comment struck a chord. The ladies turned to one another and smirked in tandem. I really didn't feel like pestering these people for the inside scoop. It wouldn't have made a difference at that point. We were nearing the city of Indio. In time, the sight of the Empire Polo Grounds would mark the horizon and we would be greeted by the sunbaked masses.

Carload after carload and busload after busload was inching into the venue. Our anticipation was peaking, so most of my friends figured *they* should start peaking— chemically speaking. Max slyly divvied out little blue pills of ecstasy to those in need. The heat was already so intense, and I was such a rookie with mind-altering substances that all I could think of was, "Everyone is always carrying around a jug of water when they're rolling on E and I'll probably pass out or die if I do this now and that would suck."

Max assured me that if I changed my mind, he'd have plenty of pills on him at the show, and he was even leaving some on the bus for the ride home. For a drug dealer, he was very sweet and considerate—two characteristics that make for shitty drug dealing. But he was also our friend, so we were grateful for his professional flaws.

After the bus stopped near the outskirts of the parking area, Santa told everyone that thirty minutes after the concert was over we were to reconvene at this exact location, that it was our responsibility to not party so hard that we couldn't find our way back to the bus, and if we were late for any reason we would be left behind. While I feared that some members of my entourage would fail to meet at least one of the said guidelines, they all agreed and we happily exited the yellow shit box.

Because Really Rockin' Buses was a loose affiliate of the concert's promoter, we managed to sneak past the enormous entrance lines, which meant I didn't have to miss any of Iggy Pop's performance. He was due to go onstage, so I broke for the main stage with Shane, Corey, and Blair while Team Hip-Hop (everyone else) hustled to a smaller stage to watch rapper Del the Funky Homosapien. No one brought cell phones, but we were confident that the same skills that helped humans locate other humans for thousands of years would lead us to a designated beer garden in one hour.

Meanwhile, retro rock band the Dandy Warhols were wrapping up their set with a butchered version of the Rolling Stones' "Jumpin' Jack Flash" that they called "Bohemian Like You." With their '60s-meets-'70s-meets-'80s clothing, they looked like every hipster in 2018, so I sorta gave them props for being ahead of their time. But they sounded bad (for any generation) and were probably better suited for smaller, darker, colder venues.

Nevertheless, they strutted off the stage to scattered

applause while a few seasoned roadies with scraggly beards and faded tats began to set the stage for rock & roll's finest physical specimen. A few years later, Iggy would headline the same stage in front of 50,000 people with the reunited Stooges. But at this point in his career, Iggy Pop was a bit of an underground legend and there were only a few hundred people awaiting his arrival. Shane, Corey, Blair, and I got so close to the stage that when Iggy exploded onto the scene we could clearly see his trademark bulging veins. We could even see some capillaries.

Iggy Pop slithered and screamed his way through the set like a leather-skinned animal on the prowl. Those were the days of aggro rap-rock bands, and a gentleman in his fifties brought more angst than a fleet of pubescent Juggalos. At the end of his lightning-charged set, Iggy further defied the limitations of old age and dove headfirst into the crowd. Before long, he was floating on his back over a sea of hands and drifting in our direction. With his eyes closed and arms calmly outstretched at his sides like Christ on the cross, Iggy detonated a massive loogie into the air. A shrapnel dab of spit found its way to my forehead and it was as if I had been baptized by the Pope.

-5-

When Iggy went off stage, we walked toward the beer garden to meet up with the rest of our crew. Some of our fake IDs worked. Some didn't. So we rebooted the standard procedure of circulating a few 21-and-older wristbands from our oldest-looking friends and handing them to our baby-faced friends on the outside of the fence. A few hiccups aside, we were all happily drinking overpriced Bud Lights and swapping stories about how great the performances had already been.

Since the vast majority of Team Hip-Hop was riding high on their ecstasy trip, they felt I really blew it by not going to see Del the Funky Homosapien, who was unquestionably the greatest artist that ever held a microphone. It's hard to argue with people who have no iris left in their eyes, so I just sipped on my beer and agreed.

Around mid-afternoon, the heat continued to rise and the crowd grew thick. While we planned to bounce around and see a number of different acts, it was tough to leave the shady patch of grass that lay beneath our asses. Max made the migration even less inviting when he busted out a bag of perfectly rolled Mexi joints. Once those got sparked, our buns were officially glued and the beer garden was where we watched the next several hours of performances. I don't even know if, or how, anyone got up to pee.

-6-

Eventually, Shane and I got bored with the Cheech and Chong pow-wow. Shane was my partner in crime and best friend since birth. Somehow, good fortune or bad karma had kept us together all the way to college. While art had always been my passion, chasing girls had been Shane's creative exploit, so the thought of wasting all his time with girls he didn't want to sleep with was too much for him to bear. Shane was the more handsome member of our duo, so I stood back and let his mojo steer us toward sexier pastures.

His *sexth* sense returned us to the main stage area, which was now teeming with emo kids and Rivers Cuomo clones who had flocked to watch Weezer do their thing. As we weaved our way through scattered packs of teenage girls that didn't quite pass Shane's inspection, he stopped short and honed his gaze.

"Bro, I totally nailed that chick last year!"

An endless line-up of nameless girls instantly scrolled through my mind, because when you lived with someone as slutty as Shane it was hard to pin the tail on the donkey. Regardless, Shane was positive that this tiny girl with freckles and dark red hair had allowed him to penetrate her before. So in a drunken flash, he danced over to her and, as is commonplace for guys who kinda look like Johnny Depp, the girl welcomed him with open arms.

Luckily, she had a cute friend who looked a little like Rosario Dawson and a lot like my type. So I held onto Shane's coattails and found myself chatting with the hotter of the two, which rarely ever happened. Thanks to MDMA, she was digging my shit from the get-go. Both girls had already consumed a ton of ecstasy and were equal candidates for horniest human ever. Shane was eager for his own nomination, so he popped a few pills that he finagled from Max. Shane then offered me one within earshot of the girls, which was nice, but I wasn't looking to go that route.

I also wasn't looking to be the buzzkill of the bunch, so I took the pill and tossed it in my mouth. However, my neurotic Italian tendencies overpowered my inner drug user and I spit the pill on the ground when no one was looking. Most of the pill dissolved in the process, but I carried on and thought nothing of it. Besides, I was already feeling great. Some hot, sexy stranger was using me like a stripper pole and the brutal desert sun had just begun its cooling descent over the neighboring mountains.

As my dance partner continued to grind away at my southern goodness, I was rudely reminded of my serious girlfriend up north in Santa Barbara. And while I longed to be an unfaithful scumbag (because this chick wasn't throwing up *any* stop signs), I just couldn't do it. Cheating on math may have come easy to me. Despite several attempts to crunch the numbers, cheating on my girlfriend just didn't add up. So I kept my mouth and genitals to myself and vowed to nail my girlfriend the millisecond I got home.

Shane, on the other hand, was single as the day he came out of his mother's womb. He had already begun a bizarre public display of affection with his lady friend that only got more bizarre. I'm telling you, the ecstasy must've been tailored to his blood type because Shane's hands were traversing her body with such passion I thought he was polishing a fucking Ferrari. Mr. Miyagi might've bowed at his wax-on technique, but I was afraid Shane was gonna whip out his dipstick and check her oil.

After yelling his name at full volume a half-dozen

times, I finally broke up the heavy petting. DJ Paul Oakenfold's set was underway at this point and the girls wanted
to head over to another stage and watch Fatboy Slim. Even
though rave music was like dry anal rape on my ears, I figured I'd wait out Paul Oakenfold and get a good spot for
Jane's Addiction, who was due up next. Shane was clearly
focused on following the Ferrari.

Before Shane took off, I felt inclined to remind my best
friend—who I had been going to concerts with since we
were thirteen years old—that he was going to miss the
greatest rock show he'd never seen for a piece of ass that
he'd already had. Somehow my words temporarily diluted
the ecstasy, because soon Shane coordinated a new rendezvous spot with the girls and he and I were stuck in a
crowd of ravers.

-7-

Spazzed-out poster children for abstinence were hopping
around me, sniffing Vicks VapoRub and pumping their
fists to unbearable dance beats. I was not the kind of guy
to wave my hands in the air like I just didn't care. In fact, I
was more inclined to start chucking fists at random dudes;
but I started to feel a little *off*.

A soft wave of euphoria washed over me with unexpected force when I should've been at my most cynical.
Whatever minor amount of ecstasy that slipped into my
saliva was transforming me into my worst nightmare: an
amateur raver. But shockingly, I welcomed the change,

pumping my fists and basking in an onslaught of strobe lights that attacked my rods and cones from the stage. It was the most epic sensory detour I'd been on since I discovered my parents' *Penthouse* magazines at age four.

I turned to Shane, who was doing some sloppy Jim Morrison rain dance, and shouted, "This is *sooooo awesome!*"

Shane pinned his forehead against mine and yelled, "Yeah, man! Magical light storms make cosmic babies and butterflies!"

I should've taken that as an indication that Shane was temporarily out of service, but I was just relieved he didn't try to make out with me. For a few more embarrassing minutes, we danced ourselves stupid, turning whatever reckless teenage angst we had saved for our twenties into something worthy of cosmic babies and butterflies—until the music finally stopped and the rave was no more.

-8-

When Paul Oakenfold's set ended, the bright house lights came on and Shane and I found ourselves just a few feet from the front of the stage. While I was stoked that we had somehow obtained the best standing seats in the house, Shane took one glance around at the thousands of people packed like sardines in sweat and had a panic attack. One second he was standing, the next he dropped to the ground and took refuge in the dark space against my shins.

Our proximity to the stage meant that we were absorbing the momentum of everyone that was pushing for a closer spot. A human riptide threatened to sweep us away, but Shane remained glued to the ground—more speed bump than man. Then, a thunderous applause filled the valley when the silhouettes of Dave Navarro, Steven Perkins, and Martyn LeNoble appeared onstage. The opening bass notes to "Up the Beach" signaled the start of Jane's Addiction's headlining performance, but it wasn't until front man Perry Farrell emerged in a white pimp suit with a bottle of red wine that the crowd really showed its enthusiasm.

Back then, you didn't have the luxury of selfish assholes recording the show from an upright, stagnant position on their phones. Instead, you had to shove everyone around you so you didn't end up trampled and dead. So, with 30,000 surging fans on my back, I grabbed Shane by the hair and yanked him to his feet.

"Hey, bro! Knock off the hide-and-go-seek shit! You are going to *die*!"

You'd think such a dire proposition would knock some sense into a person, but *no*. Death was no match for bad vibes and a handful of ecstasy. Shane just stared at me with some bugged-out expression invented by lemurs, then retreated toward the ground. While I fought to keep his dumb ass on his feet, the mellow mood of "Up the Beach" segued into the far more assertive sound of Jane's next song, "Stop." The tune should've been called "Start the Gnarliest Fucking Mosh Pit Imaginable," because that's what the people right behind us did.

With a 150-pound rag doll clinging to my arm, I tricked my own 125 pounds into carrying us both to safety. It was a pleasant few seconds, followed by the appearance of an even gnarlier mosh pit just a few feet away. Roid-raging brutes were mowing down everyone in their path, and Shane's inability to stand up like a big boy was compromising our survival. I was almost ready to say 'fuck it' and fend for myself when I felt a hand tugging on my leg.

"You've got to be shitting me, Shane!" I barked toward the ground.

To my surprise, Shane was still teetering on his own two feet. I quickly looked down and saw a pudgy face with sweat pouring off a sandpaper beard.

"Help me!" the man shrieked.

"Stand up! You're gonna get crushed!"

"I can't!"

"No, just stand up! I'll hold the people back for you!"

"I *can't stand up*!"

Now, I've got a pretty vivid imagination, but for some reason his words made no damn sense. Two legs=stand up...right? While I racked my fuzzy brain, something bizarre knocked Shane out of his stupor. He pointed overhead and I followed the coordinates of his hand. There lay the exception to my equation: A shiny silver wheelchair was floating over the audience like some armored crowd surfer. This poor dude was paralyzed!

Before I had a chance to feel like an insensitive prick, I was forced to play hero. Again, I was outweighed, but I managed to haul this guy off the ground. He reeked of fermented gym socks, but worse, he was a lot heavier perpendicular to the earth, and without some swift assistance we would *both* be immobilized. I begged for help, but everyone around us was too focused on the concert to assess our situation.

As our two-man tower began to crumble, Shane defied the laws of toxicology and sprang into action. With this guy's hairy arms wrapped around our necks, we bulldozed to the front of the stage. There, a security guard collected our weakest link and carried him away. Luckily, he was safe. Naturally, we were relieved. And fortunately, in the hundreds of other concerts I've attended since that night, I never stumbled upon another paraplegic minus a wheelchair.

-9-

As luck would have it, the rest of Jane's Addiction's set was free from any once-in-a-lifetime drama. Shane and I partied along with the thousands of other freaks who had congregated in the sweltering desert to enjoy something truly out of the ordinary. When the promoter finally pulled the plug on a mind-blowing rock show, Shane thanked me for convincing him to watch Jane's Addiction. Before I could say you're welcome, he was dragging me across the field to reconnect with Rosario and the Ferrari.

The hour of Santa's exodus was growing near, but the girls (who hadn't lost any ground in their quest for horny supremacy) insisted that we spend the night at their nearby hotel room. They even promised they would drive us back to Santa Barbara in the morning. So, basically, it would've been the same as taking Really Rockin' Buses— with a complimentary orgy.

Again, thoughts of my serious(ly inconvenient) girl-friend complicated my course of action. Shane made it clear that I was the Albert Einstein of morons if I didn't tag along. He could've lumped in Babe Ruth, Bill Gates, and Luke Skywalker, because there should've been no debate. These chicks were down for whatever and it was really up to our inner perverts to define the terms of 'whatever.' At that moment, I wanted to take a dump on my moral fiber. I wanted to wipe my ass with monogamy and bang these horny strangers.

"No, thanks. You guys have fun."

Yep, I said that. And my dick has never forgiven me for being such a pussy.

-10-

After I cut ties with Shane and the other two-thirds of his threesome, I sprinted back to Santa's rendezvous spot. There, I found the ladies of Really Rockin' Buses and the other bus riders reminiscing about various bands. Mirac-ulously, Team Hip Hop returned with all its members in tow. I soon learned that Max spoiled them with plenty of leftover ecstasy during Jane's Addiction's set, so they were *super happy* to see me. That happiness came in the form of a colossal group hug that I'm guessing only war heroes and showcase winners on *The Price is Right* have felt. When the reunion embrace loosened up, we realized that one important face was missing, besides Shane.

It seemed that Santa was late to his own departure. To make matters more annoying, the fucking bus hadn't even arrived. So, there we waited on the outskirts of the parking lot while thousands of cars set off toward homes with hot showers. Meanwhile, the wild desert winds were blasting us with dirt-ridden air that was easily forty degrees colder than the midday heat. All the serotonin in the world couldn't soothe our discomfort and tempers began to flare.

"This is fuckin' ridiculous! Where the hell is Santa?" Corey yelled.

His thin mess of black hair nearly sprouted horns as he marched over to the bus employees to interrogate them. He returned with nothing good. Santa and the ladies got separated around four o'clock and they hadn't seen him since.

But then we all saw him. Santa marched up to our group and offered a rattled apology before he pulled the ladies of Really Rockin' Buses aside for a private discussion. Two sentences in and we could see that something was up...something *bad*. The ladies' jaws fell open while Santa rambled on about God knows what. He motioned for one of their cell phones and dialed away. A look of suppressed fear pulled at his fat face, then he hung up and walked back to us.

"All right, people. Everything's fine! The bus is just having trouble getting into the parking lot, so we're going to intercept it at the entrance."

What a relief! In a few short minutes, we would be reunited with a warm change of clothes and Max's drugs. So we hustled to the outskirts of the polo field and looked for the bus. But there was no bus. There was only more wind and more dirt. Despite these facts, Santa assured us that the bus was on its way.

An endless two hours later, we had heard that the bus was just minutes away for the last time. By now, all the good energy had been exhausted from the ecstasy we consumed and an irritated mob of speed-soaked jerks was plotting a mutiny.

"I don't know who the fuck Santa was callin' on the phone, but this is complete *bullshit*! It's two in the fuckin' morning! If the bus was going to get us, it would've already been here! We're freezin' our asses off while he feeds us a bunch of fuckin' lies, and I'm *sick* of it! I say we go get the cops and have them arrest his ass for kidnappin' us!"

Although we were all thinking the same thing, it took Corey's bold words to mobilize the revolt. He topped it off by chasing after Santa and trying to beat the shit out of him before being restrained by members of our entourage. We hurled a few more insults toward the Really Rockin' Buses crew, then a bunch of college kids and high school minors went searching for the very people we feared the most—to help save us from Santa.

-11-

"So...*none* of you have transportation home?"

In his many years on duty, the veteran police officer we found patrolling the empty polo grounds had yet to encounter civilians in our situation. Sure, homicidal meth-heads popped up on a daily basis in the desert, but thirty shivering students with no means of transportation was just plain *weird*.

Rather than honor our requests to lock up Santa and send us home on a private jet, three additional officers were called to the scene to devise a more realistic solution. First, they tracked down Santa and his employees and lumped us together to figure out what really went wrong. Santa danced around the issue, offering assorted excuses and tales of miscommunication, but the cops weren't buying his bullshit—not on *their* salaries. Eventually, Santa was forced to deliver the truth.

Sometime in the late afternoon, Santa left his backpack unattended while he went to take a leak. When he came back, it was gone. If the backpack had been used to store granola bars, that would've been fine. But it just so happened to contain Santa's cell phone, which contained the driver's phone number and all the emergency documents that would've led us to the bus company if for some reason Santa's cell phone disappeared by a porta-potty.

Santa used the police phone to check if the driver had left him a voicemail, but that was not the case. The cops thought that maybe the driver had fallen asleep on the bus and was stationed somewhere nearby. The scenario we dreaded the most was that the driver had snooped through all the stuff we left behind (at least a few thousand dollars in clothing, jewelry, electronics, and narcotics) and fled his minimum-wage job with our shit. All this speculation really meant was that the most bizarre concert of our lives was going to be at least a two-day event. The cops were sorry to inform us that every hotel, motel, and Holiday Inn was sold out within fifty miles and it was too late to charter a bus home. Whatever air was left in the figurative balloon got farted out with those words.

"Well, where the hell are we going to sleep?" I asked one of the officers.

"We're working on that right now. In the meantime, we need you all to get in our vehicles and we can get you some food while we sort things out."

And with that, we piled into a variety of police vehicles and left the Coachella Valley Music and Arts Festival just *slightly* behind schedule.

-12-

Justin, Chelsea, and I were gorging ourselves with a few thousand calories of top-shelf Jack in the Box when our chauffeuring officer informed us that we would be spending the night at an elementary school. Justin was one of the first friends I made in college and I felt more at ease about our worsening situation with a buddy beside me—even though his oversized legs were crammed against my skeleton to make more room for his girlfriend. It was almost too fitting that we arrived at the concert in a school bus filled with illegal goods and we were headed to a kids' school in a cop car.

When we arrived at the Southwest-inspired institution, it was that eerie point in the day where the sun wasn't up, but it wasn't dark anymore. The cops ushered everyone into the cafeteria where absolutely no signs of cots or bed-like structures existed. There were tables fit for hobbit-sized offspring, and there were two styles of floor: hardwood and harder linoleum. However, the presence of warm running water transformed the school into a Four Seasons resort for one hot minute. The boys and girls filed into their respective bathrooms to take makeshift showers in the tiny sinks. It would take more than Dial soap and brown paper towels to wash off the effects of twenty hours of weather torture, but I gave my exposed flesh a quick scrub before returning to the cafeteria to find a stiff resting spot.

There, the police told us that Santa and the Really Rockin' Buses ladies were stashed in an undisclosed location on campus so none of us (mainly Corey) could attack them in their sleep. A few cops even stood guard in the cafeteria to make sure we didn't snoop around or trash the place. It was beginning to feel a lot more like jail than a place where CapriSuns and Lunchables were consumed.

As I curled up on a rough patch of hardwood and tried to go nite-nite, I was haunted by the thought that Shane was nearby in some posh hotel, maybe even a *real* Four

Seasons. And he was sound asleep...on pillowy mounds of boobies.

-13-

I slept for a grand total of zero minutes. Some of the high school kids' parents arrived at the cafeteria before the sandman. Obviously, they were irate that their prized possessions had not been returned to Santa Barbara and they were eager to find out why the fuck not.

Everyone was awake by the time the cops brought Santa into the cafeteria to get chewed out. It wasn't pretty. These parents laid into Santa with every ounce of anger they managed to muster during their 250-mile trip to Palm Springs, and within minutes Santa was crying for his mommy and daddy. It was then that the officers informed us that Santa was only eighteen years old.

It turned out he was just some high school tech nerd who knew how to design websites and had convinced the concert promoter that he was a professional adult. Really Rockin' Buses had made several successful tours to concert events that year, but this was likely to be their last. The words "lawsuit" and "we're gonna sue you, asshole" were tossed around more than once before the angry parents took their kids and split.

Mr. and Mrs. Claus, or whatever they were called, showed up soon after to retrieve Santa. They were a plump couple and wore their son's shame well. After a brief consolation, they whisked Santa away like they were fleeing the North Pole paparazzi. As expected, we bombarded their escape with an onslaught of boos and jeers. It was kind of a dick move. After all, the kid just made a mistake—a mistake that left many people craving court-ordered compensation, but a mistake nonetheless.

The satisfaction brought on by Santa's painful exit was short-lived, because the remaining twenty-odd people still dwelling in the communal dining area were still without a ride home. None of us had bothered to contact our parents for fear that they would find out what our tuition was really paying for. Meanwhile, the police were doing their best to get us mobile, but getting a private bus on a Sunday was apparently sacrilege in Palm Springs. So the hours dragged on with no promising leads, and day turned into afternoon and afternoon was looking a little bit like night.

By 5 p.m., hope was no longer on the cafeteria menu. The rightful heirs to the school would be arriving in the morning and we'd be hard to pass off as fifth graders with facial hair or full boobs. Then, just when we were about to bite the bullet on a fleet of $500 cab rides or a free night at the county jail, we were rescued by a knight in advertisement-covered armor.

-14-

A lone public transit bus idled in the school parking lot. It was empty and offered direct service in the direction of Santa Barbara. The latter detail meant we were getting on the fucking thing. So we thanked the officers for the wonderful dinner and deluxe accommodations and headed home with a newfound appreciation for the po-po...I mean, *officers of the law.*

An hour later, we stopped in Riverside and transferred to an older city bus whose rigid fiberglass seats were inspired by spinal distress. Thankfully, a random girl was kind enough to share her prescription of Somas and soon we were all warm and cozy in our discomfort.

Somewhere around Ventura County, I remember looking around at the people on the bus. A few lucky souls fell asleep, but most of them were too delirious to pass out. Michael, who was my closest friend that year, slowly shook his head at me when our eyes met. His face already received more color than his pale European bloodline could handle, but his cheeks turned a deeper shade of crimson as he processed the absurdity of our situation. We both began to crack up. Once we knew we were nearing the comforts of our college town, the trauma of the past two days was reduced to its comical core. If the Coachella Valley Music and Arts Festival carried on for another hundred years, no other concertgoers would experience a journey so unique, so hilarious.

-15-

A few days later, the bus that didn't pick us up was found. It wasn't stripped bare and burning in a roadside ditch in Mexico. It was back in Santa Barbara with all our shit. As the police expected, our bus driver had fallen asleep when he never heard from Santa. When he woke up in the middle of the night, he panicked and drove back to Santa Barbara. Now he was unemployed. That didn't change the fact that lawyers had been contacted and lawsuits were cooking. I thought financial retribution was only justifiable if I had been physically mutilated, so I was just happy to get my refund for the bus ride and my sweater back.

When some of my crew went to collect their belongings with dollar signs in their eyes, a cheap scenario awaited them. Somehow, Santa discovered a few dozen questionable blue pills in a backpack that contained Max's school ID card. Even though Santa had no legal right to search through his stuff, possession of just one pill of ecstasy was enough to warrant a felony. Max was in a bind. He did the smart thing and told Santa to flush any mysterious pills down the toilet because he didn't know *whose* or *what* they were. Santa's parents did the smarter thing and threatened to have the cops sort out the situation if anyone tried to sue their son. The upper hand was theirs. Max didn't even have a finger on top.

And that was the final chapter of our brief but memorable relationship with Santa. Max didn't go to jail, no one got rich, Shane started dating the Ferrari, and we all carried on with our indulgent college lives until the memory of our Coachella trip became so distorted by the elements that I sometimes wonder if we really went there at all.

But we *did* go there. *Right, guys*?

My Coachella ticket.

A RAID ON THE UNIVERSITY VAMPIRES

-1-

I was awake at 5 a.m. many times in college. I lived with
mortal vampires who were dead-set on proving that sleep
was an elective course. My party-monster roommates were
not alone in their pursuit of assisted insomnia. During my
sophomore year at UC Santa Barbara, I had been bit on
the neck by drug dealers and saw my reflection on enough
horizontal mirrors to know the veins on my forehead better
than those on the back of my hand.

Nine of us lived in a broccoli-colored two-story home
in the heart of Isla Vista—a small town that was 98% stu-
dent-occupied and 99% debauched. Several nights a
week, my roommates and I paraded the streets, drunk
and drugged-up, staggering from party to party with little
regard for the educational system that awaited us Monday
through Friday.

However, one Wednesday morning in the spring of
2001, I was asleep when I was supposed to be. Midterms

were taking place and I preferred to have my grades located at the front of the alphabet. Scholarship money followed a good report card, and buying illegal goods with money I earned felt less pathetic than using money that was given to me by my sweet, dead grandpa.

Having a studious roommate like Carl Pendleton made the process easier. A one-time social butterfly, Carl retired from having fun because his chemistry major required around-the-clock study sessions. Surveillance cameras got more rest than him. While Carl's disregard for sleep made him a good fit for our house, he somehow achieved sleeplessness without stimulants and didn't like living with guys who achieved similar results the *snorty* way. But Carl found other ways to fit in, because when *his* brain eventually demanded sleep, it needed marijuana—which our roommates, Justin and Michael, sold down the hall.

The previous year, I developed a friendship with Justin and Michael over our fondness for *Tony Hawk's Pro Skater 2*—a video game that enabled a surfer from California and two hip-hop kids from Colorado to put aside their cultural differences and waste hours of their prized youth in harmony. Justin was six-four, half-Mexican, and the product of attractive breeding. Michael was his all-white physical counterpart with more impressive sideburns. They were easygoing guys with admirable party skills, and I knew they would make awesome roommates.

When we finally moved into 6730 Del Playa Drive, which contained 700 square feet of communal space, Justin and Michael realized that our home was suitable for much greater things than playing Playstation, so they became pot dealers to improve the entertainment value of our home. At least once a week, the Del Playa pad became a twisted playground for dozens of young adults too advanced for the underwhelming Greek scene. Plenty of those visitors were pothead buddies that Justin and Michael met in the freshman dorms, and whether they had a few bucks or a hundred bucks, Justin and Michael hooked them up with the finest chronic in town. With their profits, they bought speakers, turntables, records, TVs, movies, kegs, and whatever it took to keep the party going when all the other parties ended in Isla Vista. But Justin and Michael's desire to provide a valuable community service meant that too many *bros* became household regulars.

My good buddies, Ross and Danny—twin brothers who were so identical that girls who slept with both of them couldn't tell them apart—moved back into the Del Playa pad after three months in a study-abroad program. Like Carl, they too liked weed. Unfortunately, discounted dope didn't make living in the new stoner Mecca of UC Santa Barbara a fair trade. Before long, the tension in our once tight-knit household was higher than the hippies passing through our halls. Arguments erupted daily and I had trouble picking sides. Justin and Michael were the best friends I made in college. Our casual video game engagements turned into months of inseparable bonding where we lived together like brothers. I spent less time around Ross and Danny, but I respected them and they had a valid excuse for being upset. They didn't want to live in a twenty-four-hour marijuana convenience store. Neither did I.

After a house meeting where everyone voiced their concerns, Justin and Michael agreed that marijuana trans- actions would only be offered to a select number of friends. Stock prices for Ziploc baggies probably took a dive that month, but Justin and Michael kept their word and cus- tomer foot traffic slowed. Then, early that fateful Wednes- day morning, the foot traffic appeared to be back in step.

-2-

I woke from a sober sleep to the sound of our front door opening downstairs. A small digital alarm clock on my nightstand radiated 5:01 a.m. in green lights. Carl was asleep across the room with his thin face and dirty blond hair smushed against a pillow. He had returned from the library an hour earlier, but I didn't mind when he came home late. Carl was quiet and light-footed in his move- ments. However, my wasted roommates and their entou- rage ran through the ground floor with heavy Franken- stein feet. My annoyance intensified as they sprinted up the stairs to their respective bedrooms. Based on their energized behavior, I knew they weren't going to hit the hay. They were likely going to hit the sauce and bump rap music until one of the non-partying roommates was kind enough to tell them to shut the fuck up.

I closed my eyes and prayed I could go back to sleep, but my prayers were outmatched. My roommates were hollering nonsense as they came up the stairs. Through my closed door, it sounded like, "It's a rave! It's a rave! It's a rave!" That meant they were rolling on ecstasy and they would be too happy to sense my displeasure. As the foot-steps drew closer to my bedroom, a voice yelled out, "It's a rave!" one last time. Only now, the voice was not distorted by distance and it sounded just like, "*It's a raid!*"

A deafening explosion roared through my room as my Masonite door burst into toothpicks and flew off the hinges. A towering figure stepped through the doorway dressed in head-to-toe SWAT team gear. He had a long automatic weapon pointed in my direction with a red laser darting out from the scope. A lone demon pupil drew the mark of death on my chest as he raced up to me and threw me onto the floor. Another well-armed man—pasty white with his head shaved clean to the scalp—entered the room and gave Carl the same good-morning treatment.

We lay face down on our filthy carpet, clothed only in boxer shorts, with large knees blanketing our backs. As handcuffs clamped down on our wrists, I could hear government warriors yanking my other roommates out of their beds and breaking everything in their paths. It didn't matter that none of us had weapons. These guys treated us with the same respect as vigilante *narcos* on a Netflix show.

"Where are the fucking drugs?" shouted the officer resting on top of my spine.

"I don't know!" I squealed.

He disliked my answer and tossed me back on the bed where he stared at my terrified twenty-year-old face with a vicious mid-thirties scowl. He appeared to be of Native

American descent, tan-skinned with a braided ponytail draped over his shoulder. The officer shifted his dark eyes to my dyed black hair, earrings, and tattoos. I was a dread-lock away from being the poster child for college burnouts and he knew I had to be a druggie to alter my appearance so poorly.

"Don't fucking lie to me! Where are you hiding your drugs, kid?"

"I told you, man," I paused, fearing the worst as I continued to tell the truth, "I don't have any."

His face filled with offensive delight. I wished I had a kilo of drugs taped to my forehead to pacify this lunatic, but I never carried drugs. I was too paranoid for weed, too high-strung for psychedelics, too scared of heroin, and too cheap to buy more than a night's supply of cocaine. The officer assumed otherwise and threw my nearby desk on its side. He peered at the jumbled mess of books and paperwork, expecting drugs to rise like cream to the top of the pile. To his dismay, nothing caught his eye, not even my two fake IDs that were peeking out of an art history essay.

He then moved to Carl's side of the room and unload-ed the entire contents of our walk-in closet on the floor. Clothing of all kinds, CDs, video cassettes, and sports gear flew off of shelves. Again, I was shocked by how little the guy inspected our mounting pile of crap for drugs. He basically taught us how to throw an award-winning tan-trum, ten years too late. But his housekeeping scare tactics were too much for Carl, who wasn't going to wait for the officer to attack his nearby mid-term assignments.

"Officer, I have a pipe and some weed under my bed," he muttered.

In a half-blink, the bald officer flipped Carl's mattress from its cinderblock frame and discovered a tiny glass pipe and a nug of weed—street value maybe five bucks. While he appraised the measly stash, the other officer sat Carl's lanky body in a chair and got right in his face.

"You mean to tell me that's *all* you've got, buddy?"

"Yes, it is," he responded in a lifeless, whispery tone, seemingly unfazed by the presence of an angry man with a machine gun.

To the unfamiliar ear, Carl sounded like he had fried a considerable amount of his brain due to heavy drug use. I actually grew up with Carl and knew that was not the case. He was pretty bizarre, but not a burnout. The officer believed he was the latter, especially when he got a good look at Carl's mysterious blue eyes.

"Your pupils are the size of quarters! Cut the bullshit! Where's the coke? Where's the ecstasy?"

"I don't know what you're talking about. I don't do hard drugs. Only pot."

The officer stepped back, tugging on his ponytail, trying to curb his frustration.

"Okay, buddy, this is your last chance to tell me where you're hidin' the other drugs, or we will tear this room to pieces!"

Again, Carl claimed he didn't do hard drugs; and again the cops heard a drug user telling a big, fat lie. As the officers moved about the room, happy to continue their unruly home make-over, I saw Carl cringe in anticipation. The consequences of his honesty seemed completely unjust so I spoke up in his defense.

"Officers, I swear he doesn't do hard drugs! He's just...*a little off.*"

"Explain," the bald cop demanded.

"Well, he's been studying almost non-stop for two weeks."

"*So?*"

"So, maybe he's gone crazy," I said.

The other cop kneeled before Carl, curiously reviewing his massive pupils.

"You don't even do Adderall? Or Ritalin?"

"No. Not at all."

Carl's deadpan response was free from any signs of stimulant intake. Nonetheless, the officer pulled out a flashlight and conducted an eye exam. While Carl's eyes followed the wandering light perfectly, the officer was dumbstruck by the results. The other cop swooped in and administered several more tests until Carl—the inconsequential pawn in a college drug bust—became their wildest discovery of all time.

"I've never seen anything like him!"

"I know! His pupils hardly get smaller when I take away the flashlight."

"He must have developed some abnormal light sensitivity."

"You're not a mutant, are you, kid?"

The officers laughed out loud, slapping their thighs at

what I surmised was cutting-edge cop humor. After the lame joke fizzled out, they decided the rest of the SWAT team needed to experience their prized freak. Carl was not consulted on the matter, but he was taken away and I was left alone with Baldy.

Since I was just a guy with normal pupils, the cop wanted absolutely nothing to do with me. He started moping around and let out an overdramatic sigh as though he had been assigned a lifetime of issuing jaywalking tickets. When he neared the area where my fake IDs landed, I really regretted buying those phony pieces of shit.

Sometime in the summer, I purchased two licenses for eighty bucks from a guy that specialized in making New Mexico IDs. Why New Mexico? I still have no fucking clue. Why two IDs? I recall there was not an option to buy a single license, which should've been a warning that they were so bad that one would be confiscated by the first person who carded me and the second would serve as a reminder that I had been ripped off. Each license showcased my photo and false information adhered to a plastic card with a black stripe across the back that had no information imbedded into the surface.

The reason I still had both of them in my possession was because I only visited bars and liquor stores that catered to underage alcoholics. Getting caught with fake IDs was a costly misdemeanor with potential jail time. Both penalties seemed to outweigh the benefits of all the Miller High Life I purchased as the cop came within inches of my IDs. But just as he seemed to take notice of their poorly rendered hologram surfaces, the officer stopped short and his attention shifted to a painting hanging proudly on the wall. The piece was the undeniable standout of my midterm portfolio and it featured an assortment of detailed portraits of my friends. The man appeared to be quite taken by its beauty. Then, without a second thought, he pulled out a long folding knife and took a stab at the painting. My paternal instincts kicked in before the blade pierced the canvas and I screamed at him as if he were attacking my child.

"What the fuck are you doing, dude? That's my fuckin' painting! Don't fuckin' cut it!"

The officer's head whipped back, surprised by my vocal onslaught. Knives aside, this guy was twice my size and could've beat the shit out of me with his pinkie finger; yet, he appeared to shrink in stature with every curse-laden sentence I fired his way.

"I'm sorry!" he shouted. "I've heard that people store drugs behind pictures."

"*Really*? Well, it weighs less than a pound. Put the fuckin' knife away and take it off the goddamn wall if you want to check it for drugs!"

The officer didn't bother to check for a mountain of narcotics stashed behind a half-inch thick painting. He folded his knife on command and tried to patch things up with his captive artist.

"I just want you to know that I deeply respect art," he said, then waited for my blood to return to a stable simmer. "This is a nice painting. Is this oil or acrylic?"

"*Acrylic*," I growled, officially putting an end to our artistic discussion.

I may have been handcuffed, but I was in control of the room. The power shift proved to be short-lived. The other officer returned, uninterested in discussing the aesthetic differences between oil and water-based pigments. He grabbed me by the shoulder and walked me out of the room.

"Am I going to jail?" I cautiously asked.

The man grunted through his nose then tightened his already firm grip. "That depends."

-3-

I rounded the blind corner of our L-shaped stairway, heading downstairs with the officer trailing me. When I came upon the living room, I found all of my roommates seated on our collection of hand-me-down couches. If I looked past the handcuffs and cheap furniture, I would've thought I was entering a funeral parlor. Long, sad faces barely clung to their skulls. A few faces were seeped in anger—namely Ross, Danny, and Carl. Their college lives were the least enriched by the pot-sponsored parties that led up to the raid and now they were probably facing misdemeanor drug charges.

I was eager to know if we all were looking at criminal records and expulsion from school as I sat beside Carl on our stained pullout. The SWAT team approached this operation very seriously. A dozen policemen wandered the home with large paper bags. Only these bags didn't say 'Whole Foods' in happy green font. They said SANTA BARBARA POLICE DEPARTMENT in scary black letters and the officers filled them with anything remotely drug related like they were contestants on *Supermarket Sweep*.

Meanwhile, a stocky Latino officer with a patchy, almost pubescent mustache emerged from the neighboring kitchen. He couldn't have been much older than us and he grinned at everyone a long time like he was imagining us spoiled college kids defending our virgin assholes in the jailhouse shower. With his grin intact, he pointed at Ross and ordered him to go into the kitchen.

When Ross came back a few minutes later, he was trembling so badly I could actually tell the difference between him and his twin brother. Either the cops stuck his head in the freezer, or a room-temperature discussion caused this reaction. After he left the group, I could faintly hear Ross talking to someone, but I couldn't make out their conversation. My curiosity strove for honor roll status when Carl was told to leave the room. I inched to the edge of the couch, tilted my head at the kitchen, and cupped my ear with discreet perfection. But again, I couldn't make out a damn word. As curiosity turned to paranoia, the little voice inside my head started yapping away.

Hey! Why do you think Ross was freaking out when he came out of the kitchen?

"He was probably just scared," I silently told myself.

Nuh-uh! He's gotta be the fuckin' narc!

"You really think so?"

Yeah! I bet he told the cops that Carl would back him up since he hated living here more than anyone.

"Wait a second, you idiot! If Ross was the narc, the cops would've told him to spend the night somewhere else. I can hear them destroying his room right above me. He's obviously not getting preferential treatment."

Oh, shit! You're right! That means one of Justin and Michael's customers got busted and gave the cops enough dirt on them to get a search warrant.

"Exactly!"

I shook my fist with pride. Then I remembered all of the jailable offenses I performed in the presence of potential snitches. The little voice inside my head fled the country. My faint morning breath turned into a nauseous gas. A Pepto-Bismol keg-stand couldn't calm the sickness brewing inside me, yet all I could do was sit quietly while neurosis sublet my digestive system.

After Carl came back, I tamed my nausea long enough to draw his attention with a cough. From there, I covertly mouthed, "What's going on in there?"

Carl waited until the coast was clear, then he whispered the following word: "*Interrogation.*"

Now it was clear what the officer meant by "It depends." He wanted me to snitch on Justin and Michael...my new best friends.

-4-

How disloyal will a friend be to protect their clean record

and, more importantly, to prevent moving back in with their parents? Those were the two issues plaguing my mind as my time to enter the dreaded kitchen became more pressing. Across the room, the morning sun sliced through a small tear in the blinds, which meant it was around 7:00 a.m. and I was the only roommate that hadn't been questioned by the police. Everyone else sat around with lousy poker faces, masking whatever emotional response they had to the interrogation process as best they could.

Then the back door of the living room swung open and in came a very unexpected guest: our dear friend Corey. He had a grey hoodie draped around his familiar boyish face, but to me and everyone not wearing a bulletproof vest, he looked like a rat. Corey always bought weed at the Del Playa pad and had enough dirt on us to fertilize the entire world. He also distributed weed in his apartment complex and it was just a matter of time before he would find himself in a desperate situation with the law. By tattling on Justin and Michael, Corey provided the cops with two higher-profile dealers and likely spared himself jail time for his own offenses.

When Corey caught sight of all the people he betrayed, he actually had the nerve to smile. Did I say he looked like a rat? What I meant to say was, he looked like a disease-ridden, tick-covered, buck-toothed rat dragging his smashed-up genitals in a rusty rat trap. I wanted to bitch-slap the smile off his face so badly that the skin underneath my handcuffs ached as my hands went into attack position. But before I could rearrange Corey's facial features, his smile deteriorated on its own. A highly caffeinated officer grabbed ahold of him and gave him a seismic shake.

"What are you doing here?"

"Uhh…I just came to, uh, give my friend his essay."

Corey unveiled several typed pages shaking in his hand. Across the room, a gravelly voice blurted out, "Oh, fuck!" I looked over and saw Warren nervously sink into the folds of a recliner. Warren was a quasi-gangster who suffered from an assortment of learning disabilities and required full-service tutoring. This meant that Corey was not a rat. He was just another unfortunate fly that landed in a black widow's web. Any other day, he would have delivered Warren's ghostwritten essay without incident. Obviously, this was the least typical day in a household that, up until 5:01 a.m., prided itself on being different. After the officer glanced at the papers, he waited until the tension in the room turned gelatinous before issuing a verdict.

"I believe you," he announced.

With one joyous sigh, Corey emptied a full tank of anxiety into the air. My roommates and I savored his good fortune as he backpedaled to safety and erased his co-starring role in our awful reality show. But Corey's legs turned to stone when the cop neglected to unleash his grip.

"Do you mind if I search you before you leave?" he asked, though it really wasn't a question.

Corey was so taken aback, he didn't stop to think about his rights, and the words, "Yeah, sure" rolled off his tongue and hung in the air like a bad fart. The officer slid his prickly hand inside Corey's chest pocket. Out came a clear plastic bag with traces of a powdery substance lining the interior. Corey's face turned whiter than an albino ghost covered in sunscreen.

As the officer hovered his nose above the not-so-mysterious bag, he proclaimed, "It's cocaine!" To my knowledge, the word 'cocaine' had never been said with such excitement in our house before. On the other hand, the word had never brought a young man to tears. Sadly, by the time Corey was handcuffed and seated on our puffy brown ottoman, his eyes were lactating.

Poor, poor Corey. He must've pulled an all-nighter writing Warren's essay and walked behind our house where the cops didn't park their cars. His seizing officer failed to inform him what was taking place, but Corey was no dummy. He knew we weren't half-naked and handcuffed because we failed to pay our internet bill. He knew we were being raided. He also knew he was probably going to jail. And I was about to find out if I would be going with him.

"Hey, kid with the earrings!" said the cop with the shit-eating grin. "You're next!"

The day had gone from completely fucked to fucked times infinity. If Justin and Michael hadn't been sidetracked by greed, this whole disaster could've been avoided. Even without drug money, we would've had plenty of fun at the Del Playa pad. Better parties throughout our college's history surely took place with lousier sound systems. My friends didn't seem too concerned with their prized possessions at that point. They were trapped in a daytime nightmare, too terrified to look at anyone or acknowledge any wrongdoing.

As I raced toward the kitchen, I couldn't bring myself to look at them either. I didn't want them to see me turn into a rat.

-5-

All the cops' intimidation methods failed to evoke as much fear as the lone woman seated calmly at our dinner table. Far more *-man* than *wo-* was this woman. Her bulging forearms would have looked out of place on Popeye. Her broad shoulders could only fit through doorways when she side-stepped. Her proper profession was linebacker for the Raiders, but her gender led her to another team: the SWAT team. She greeted me with a flatulent ray of stink-eye, then motioned for me to sit across from her.

"My name is Officer Killroy," she said, then opened a folder with several documents and informed me that I was in a lot of trouble. "Mr. Mars, we've been monitoring this house for several weeks and we have detailed audio recordings of you and your roommates using and selling drugs."

"*You do?*"

"That is correct."

"Oh."

"Now, I'm prepared to inform your university of your behavior, *unless* you are willing to cooperate with me."

I wanted to spill the beans faster than a taco truck in a

tornado. Forget about protecting my painting from a knife; Officer Killroy was about to jab a knife right through my future.

"Well, what do you want to know?"

She readied a recording device and squashed a red button with her thumb.

"Tell me what you know about your roommates' marijuana operation."

The tornado appeared to shift its course. Hell, I welcomed all of the perks of Justin and Michael's greed. I couldn't rat them out.

"I don't smoke pot, ma'am. So I don't really know much about that."

"I don't buy it."

"Well, it's true."

"You have a Rolling Stones logo tattooed on your arm and you *don't* smoke marijuana?"

"They were my favorite band the day I turned 18. It seemed like a good idea at the time," I said, laughing.

She didn't laugh. Instead, she slammed her palm on the table, nearly pulverizing the faux-wood finish.

"I have no patience for that kind of response! Now, do you want to have this conversation back at the station?"

"Nuh-nuh, ma'am."

"Good! Then tell me about your roommates' marijuana operation, *now*."

I didn't know where to start. I wanted to configure a statement that would satisfy her and spare my friends, but I just mumbled in circles.

"Trying to save your friends won't do you any good. Do you really think your friends would protect you if they were in your position?" Then she laughed in an evil, high-pitched voice that stung my earholes. I pondered her question as I winced. When Officer Killroy finally shut her nearly lipless mouth, I was prepared to tell her what she wanted to hear.

"You really wanna know the truth about my room-mates?"

She looked at me the way a bully looks at a nerd hold-ing a lunch tray.

"I can't stand them!" I shouted. "They're not my friends! I found this place on the university's housing website and I would've moved out, but I can't get off the lease. As soon as I come home from school, I go straight to my room and keep to myself. So whatever illegal stuff you claim goes on in this place, I seriously don't know about it."

My hot pile of lies could've passed a polygraph. I hon-estly believed that Justin and Michael would've spared me if they were in my position, and giving her an honest account of my roommates' marijuana business—after plenty of people had already been questioned—would've been like topping an ice cream sundae with guacamole.

"Mr. Mars, I know you've smelled marijuana being smoked in this house," she said, not sounding the least bit convinced that I wasn't full of shit, "because according to our records, this kind of behavior goes on all the time."

"Well, here's the thing. I'm not..."

"Stop stalling!"

"But I..."

"Mr. Mars, this is your *last* chance!"

Officer Killroy's ears pinned back, and for a moment I saw the black of her uniform bleed into the brown of her skin and she was a Doberman ready to snap. It was time to come clean.

"Ma'am, the truth is, I've smelled less pot here than I smelled in my parents' house. My dad has the goddamn Zig-Zag man tattooed on his arm. Got it? And thanks to the D.A.R.E. program, I nearly turned my parents in to the cops when I was a kid. I mean, do you have any idea how hard it was trying to have a normal childhood when your parents were drug addicts?"

That part wasn't bullshit and I delivered it with emotional baggage I hadn't unpacked in over a decade. Officer Killroy observed me, waiting for me to break character. I could've cried at no extra charge, but I kept my composure. She switched off the recorder and began writing in her folder. I thought I had spilled the wrong can of beans and she was going to ask me for my home address so she could bust my parents. When she lifted her head, I saw all the toughness drain from her face. Sadness filled in the cracks.

"I'm sorry, kid. I grew up with parents like that, too," she confessed.

This was not the appropriate place to exchange hugs, though she needed one more than I did. I was still handcuffed. Officer Killroy was still an officer.

She told me to go join my friends in the other room.

-6-

Soon after my interrogation, the cops took Justin and Michael away. Everyone else was spared, even Corey. The lucky roommates quickly headed upstairs to assess the final damages. Justin and Michael's room drew the most curiosity. It was destroyed to the best of the officers' abilities and only recognizable by the smell of spilled bong water. There were holes in the walls, computers on the floor, and broken DJ equipment everywhere. I had trouble believing this was the backdrop for some of the most memorable days of my life. I remembered the night in November when I was out on the deck and I met Laura, the first girl that I loved who loved me back. I remembered lying on the floor after I saw Radiohead at the Greek Theater and zoning out to their latest record. I remembered the morning my mom told me my dad nearly died of heart failure and I cried on the phone while Michael consoled me. I felt a similar pain as I walked through the wreckage. College was on life support.

When I returned to my bedroom, the space looked clean by comparison. Ten housekeepers and a gallon of Super Glue was all it needed. Carl already had his backpack readied and set off for the library. No surprise there.

After I put on some clothes and sorted through my stuff, I noticed my fake IDs still hiding in my art history essay. Two mini-mugshots smiled up at me. Next thing I knew, I was down the street buying a case of Miller High Life.

My last remaining fake ID.

HAPPY BELATED HIGH SCHOOL

-1-

Five days after my dad died, it was Valentine's Day. I didn't blame Cupid for his death, but nonetheless, love had left me with a different kind of hole in my heart. With no arrow to plug the wound, I took my bleeding innards down to the emergency room I called a dive bar and began to medi- cate, heavily.

A few months earlier, it was Christmas. College was over; so was grad school. I was 29 years old and reaping the financial rewards of two art degrees while living in Los Angeles as a starving artist. As usual, I came home to Laguna Beach to steal some holiday calories. What was unusual was that my food-friendly father looked more like me in the waistline than Saint Nick. Diet and exercise were offensive words in Bob Mars' vocabulary, which meant that something even more disrespectful was slimming him down.

On New Year's Eve, he learned that stage four pancreatic cancer was his unholy personal trainer. Forty days later, he was dead and my appetite for anything, edible or emotional, pretty much died with him. Except for alcohol. That was still alive and well. So, I decided to stuff my sorrows at the same bar my dad had received a lifetime ban from for tossing someone through the front window nearly forty years prior. I was a little less dramatic in my drunken outbursts and chose to channel my rage that evening by staying glued to a barstool.

In a small town like Laguna, word gets around without the help of social media, and my friends that visited the Sandpiper Lounge were aware that I was going through some heavy shit. However, the holiday vibe was still emanating from the patrons as they filtered in, in love or looking for it. I tried not to rain on their parade, so I kept my attention focused on my Jack and Cokes and made sure the ice cubes never got too lonely.

After a few of my buddies got tired of keeping an eye on my mood, they headed to the dance floor to look for able bodies. That would've been my strategy under normal circumstances. My commendable dance skills were responsible for more casual sex than my personality, looks, or money had ever got me, cumulatively. But dancing was something I learned from my mom. Drinking whiskey was my dad's moonwalk. So I stuck to that.

Thankfully, dive bars have a convenient way of throwing anti-socials a bone. Everyone has to pass through the barflies to get a beverage at some point. Somewhere between cocktails two and ten, a familiar tall redhead with a mesmerizing set of cat-like eyes lit up my periphery. She was the girl from my past that got away that I never *actually* got. Not because she was stuck-up or out of my league, but because I was simply too stupid to talk to her in high school.

Ten years and three diplomas later, I figured I had the credentials to make an educated move. Plus, the phrase "You've got nothing to lose" really makes sense when your soul is in the gutter. So when she saddled up to the bar, I gave her a polite smile and offered to buy her a drink. She returned both gestures and we struck up a conversation.

Since high school, she and I had talked briefly on a few occasions, but the emphasis was always on brevity. I really knew nothing about her other than the superficial basics, and that's all she knew about me. But soon, two familiar mysteries were catching up at close range on the most romantic of holidays.

As our drinks grew low and others came to the rescue, I felt the urge to push the conversation to a more honest place. Something about watching someone die makes you reconsider your present. It's always fleeting, yet it's always ripe for a bold move. So, I chose to say what was on my mind a long, long time ago.

"I know this might sound a bit weird, but I'm in a really strange emotional place right now. My dad died of cancer a few days ago."

"Oh, I'm so sorry!"

"It's okay. He actually lived an amazing life. Most people aren't so lucky. But what I'm realizing now is that life is here for the taking. And if you don't take control of your reality, then you're probably missing out on a lot of great things."

"Totally."

"So, I just wanted to tell you that I had *such* a crush on you in high school, and I really feel like an idiot for not asking you out, or at least getting to know you better when I had the chance."

I paused to take a pull from my drink and observe what happens when people hear completely honest things. She looked more flattered than creeped out. But then again, I didn't really know her well enough to pinpoint her state of intrigue.

"I mean, I just wanted to let you know that there was a period in my life when I thought you were the most beautiful girl around, and I figured you should know that," I said.

She was taken aback, for sure. And then it dawned on me. "I *thought* you *were* the most beautiful girl..." My piss-poor use of grammar had jumbled my intentions and now she was some over-the-hill hag. It was clearly a sentence fit for a backhand slap.

"Why are you telling me this?" she asked with a look of upset confusion. "I have a boyfriend."

Phewwwww. It wasn't me. It was *her*! She got my gist, but life had simply got in the way—which was better than her thinking that she was once hot, now not.

"Well, again, I just wanted to let you know."

She said thanks; then awkwardness began to butt in, so she said goodbye and disappeared into the crowd. Why she wasn't with her boyfriend on Valentine's Day was a bit curious. Maybe he was out of town on business. Adults have lives. Teenagers are always around. Anyway, I didn't trip too long over the possibilities of her romance. I had made my peace, and that was that.

When I returned to my cocktail, a hand plopped on my shoulder and spun me around. It wasn't the male member of her relationship. It was her. Before I could get out a word, she came at me like a horny fastball and hit me with her mouth. I connected with her and we ripped into a passionate kiss that clobbered any thoughts of death for a lengthy ten seconds. *One-one-thousand, two-one-thousand, three-one-thousand, four-one-thousand, five-one-thousand, six-one-thousand, seven-one-thousand, eight-one-thousand, nine-one-thousand, ten-one-thousand.*

When she finally pulled away, I yanked her back for one more memorable smooch, then released her back into the present while I savored something that should've happened at prom. Or at a keg party.

-2-

Shortly after I paid my tab, I decided to head home on foot. As I cheerfully strolled past the neighboring Jack in the Box restaurant, a tractor beam pulled me in for a greasy reward. A number of people I went to high school with were inside, looking to extend the evening with burgers, fries, and maybe a one-night stand. Several of the late-night eaters just happened to be the biggest chick magnets and brawl-

ers from my old football team. Time had made them considerably less appealing to the female population, but I
figured their pleasure for punishment had picked up the
load.

While I peered up at the glowing menu, debating over
an Ultimate Cheeseburger or a Spicy Crispy Chicken Sandwich, I noticed my friend Brian talking with one of the row-
dier upperclassmen from back in the day. Brian was clearly
hammered—eyes smashed to slits, legs weaving under the
weight of his loaded belly—and getting a little too comfortable for his own good. I saw him remove a baseball cap
from a guy named Mitchell and wave it around like a kid
toying with an over-sized puppy. Unfortunately, Mitchell
was a pit bull at heart. Along with his buddy Zane, the most
feared senior football star when I was an insignificant
freshman, they were the last guys you wanted to fuck with
that night. Luckily, Zane was patrolling the outside patio,
and as far as I could tell, was unaware of Brian and Mitchell's exchange. Mitchell and I had a fairly decent rapport
that spawned from our days surfing the same beaches in
middle school, so I tried my best to block Brian's ass-kick-
ing before it officially arrived.

"Brian, that's not your hat! Give it back, man," I said.

"Dude, I'm just messing around!"

"Adam, you better chill out your boy!" Mitchell said.
"He doesn't know me well enough to pull this shit!"

"Brian, did you hear that?"

"*Duuuuuude*! *I'm just messing around*!"

"Mitchell, please don't kick his ass. He's not really an

asshole. He's just an idiot."

I could see Mitchell's eyes boil over. Brian was shit out of luck, and that was that. Then, in a flash, Brian sensed his fate. He returned the hat and offered his most sincere apology.

"Dude, I'm fucking hammered. My bad, bro."

Eloquent? Maybe not. But it turned down the heat on Mitchell, and he headed outside to talk with Zane and let Brian keep his teeth. When the coast was clear, Brian mumbled some apologetic gibberish in my direction, then I finally decided to order a Spicy Crispy Chicken Sandwich.

A few minutes later, my deep-fried preservative-rich birdie on a bun arrived. I bit into it, burning my mouth in the process, but I didn't care. I was too busy reflecting on the beautiful randomness of my encounter with the girl that got away. Maybe we weren't meant to be together in high school. We weren't soulmate material. Kids put too much effort into relationships when they're younger and usually get way more grief than good. This was fast and over, and it felt good.

Soon my meal was reduced to crumbs and it was time to call it a night. Brian headed toward the exit and I followed his lead. Meanwhile, I couldn't stop replaying the kiss in my head. Once I got home to my depleted family, it would be hard to keep happy. Normally, I would find my dad awake at his computer, playing war games and winding down with a joint. We would shoot the shit about the details of the night and he would listen, and laugh, and praise me for my casual encounter. Well, not anymore.

Still, despite his absence, I was all smiles as I left the restaurant. Brian and I passed through the front door and then, for some strange reason, I was *airborne*. My world became a slow-motion daze of passing colors and sounds. I was parallel with the ground and positioned like a sunbather perched on his side. But it was February and freezing, so why was my body in this odd position? I could see the concrete floor moving below me and I could hear girls begin to scream as I flew through the night sky. And then I was falling. *One-one-thousand, two-one-thousand...*

I tried to brace for impact, but my preferred hand was stuck in my jacket pocket. It struggled to slip free, then somehow tore through the pocket and caught my fall—very poorly. From the bottom, I glanced up and saw Zane staring down at me with his fists cocked and loaded. Mitchell was behind him instigating a retreat. A crowd of blurry faces floundered behind them. Brian suddenly appeared overhead, scared and asking if I was alright. The human puzzle pieces began to fuse into a cohesive event. I had just taken a punch from the toughest guy in my high school. And this wasn't just any punch. It was an undetected cold-cock to the side of my face that landed with enough force to launch me into orbit. I should've been hospital-bound with a concussion or a cracked skull, or worse. A future of feeding tubes and sign language was in the cards.

One of the hysterical cashiers gauged the severity of the attack and called the police. Mitchell, to his credit, began to chastise his buddy for hitting me instead of Brian. I wasn't supposed to take that punch. But I took it, and everyone knew it was bad.

Mitchell and Zane fled on foot as the sounds of wailing cop cars drew near.

-3-

When the police arrived, I was already on my feet. And I felt...*fine*. Not as fine as that lucky son-of-a-bitch Brian, but I didn't feel like I took the punch of a lifetime. In several other encounters with lesser fists, my head had mutated much worse. In fact, only a small red blemish on my cheek was proof that I had been attacked. My grandmother's lipstick left more of a mark.

After some brief tests from the police, they concluded that I wasn't in need of immediate medical attention. Then they asked if I wanted to press charges. I declined. I realized my karma for hooking up with another man's girl on Valentine's Day had been delivered, and that was enough.

The next morning, I also realized that a proud sinner like my dad had somehow made it into Heaven. Guardian angels can sure take a punch.

Outside the Sandpiper Lounge. Jack in the Box in the distance.

MEETING A GIRL ON CLOUD NINE

-1-

"This flight is gonna suck."

Those words slipped off my shaky lips with a sincerity that sarcasm can't fake. As a sweet-faced flight attendant handed me a barf bag built for an exorcism, I thought maybe I shouldn't have stayed up until 5 a.m. drinking whiskey and pickle juice shots in Manhattan. And maybe I could skydive to the Betty Ford Clinic before we landed in LA.

I had come to New York for the biggest art show of my career: a 200-square-foot storefront on the Lower East Side that garnered zero sales. Not to be dissuaded by the size of the gallery and my growing debt, I made getting wasted my index for success. At the end of my business trip, I was a triumphant mess. All fine and dandy while you're blacked out and dancing with drunk chicks in Chelsea. Not so good when you're stumbling back to seat 18D on an airplane seconds before takeoff and trying not to lose weight the gross way.

My only comfort was that I had a whole row to myself. Divine intervention in the form of pleather chairs was all I could think about. Somewhere, God must've said "Let this poor dude return home with enough space to moan, groan, and decompress from a week of debauchery that was memorable, forgettable, and everything in between."

And then I saw her. Sitting like a beautiful damper in my plans for fetal comfort was Miss 18F. At first glance, she seemed too pure and innocent for my row. She wore white cotton pants and a soft white sweater—an angel's attire. By the time I sat down, radiating a cologne of cigarettes and booze from my dirty outfit, I figured she'd be more pissed off by my presence than I was by hers. I know we weren't in first class, but hell, she deserved better than *me*.

After a relatively bumpy takeoff, I broke the ice and told her that if I start making weird noises I'm not dying, I'm just deadly hungover. She smiled and curiously inquired about the root of my stupidity. I made small talk and told her that several hours ago I was doing what 21-year-olds are supposed to do on vacation, but that I was 31. And that was it for a few hundred miles. I slipped on my sunglasses and prayed that I'd get some much-needed rest for the remainder of the flight. Thankfully, I can't sleep on planes.

Before long, Miss 18F felt I was worthy of more small talk. She asked about what I do, what I was doing in New York, etc., etc.—simple questions that make one seem like less of a pain when they make you get out of your seat to use the bathroom. I assessed it as nothing more. But when

I discovered that we were both artists, my liver suddenly stopped aching and I started to care less about catching Zs and cared more about playing 20 Questions.

Soon, talk of the Surrealist masters, the fruits of French culture, and the fickle state of contemporary art was flying between our buffer seat. Nothing seemed awkward, nothing seemed forced, and I knew this girl was special.

Scratch that. She was amazing. That soft shell of innocence I had seen upon first inspection gave way to layers of character. She was super smart, teetering on the brink of brilliant, with a wild streak that turned me on more than I let on at the time. In my opinion, good conversation is better than good sex. Or it's certainly a lot harder to find. And considering that I was in New York to showcase a series of nude portraits of the many ex-flings I had amassed in recent years, I suddenly felt all those ladies slipping down the ranks.

With every new topic of discussion, I grew more convinced that she was too good to be true. Someone who shared a similar philosophy on life as myself, but had a brand of ambition, attitude, and allure all her own was right in front of me, with nowhere to go for the next few hours. All the online daters in the world would never be so lucky.

Then I got up to take a whiz. By the time I returned to 18D, ready to pick up where we left off and journey to some place new, Miss 18F was nose-deep in her computer, tying off some loose business ends. No matter how badly I wanted to continue our conversation, I didn't panic. She clearly liked me enough to allow our chit-chat to blossom. I figured it was only a matter of moments before she'd turn to her left and the epic dialogue would resume. But it didn't.

Seconds of silence turned into minutes, and minutes felt like hours, and she kept hammering away at the keys while I kicked myself for not having a bigger bladder. We still had thousands of miles of open air, yet all I could see was defeat. Had we met in a bar and the conversation run dry, I would've moved on and talked to someone else. But we were on an airplane, in the same row, with an open middle seat, on a flight that required more than a metric ton of luck just for me to make. Coincidence? I think not.

-2-

After I awoke on the cold kitchen floor of my friend Aaron's West Village apartment earlier that day, I discovered I had lost more than my love for whiskey. My cell phone was gone. My wallet was missing. Thankfully, I found a credit card and my license in my jeans or my chances of getting to the airport, and more importantly through post-9/11 security, would've been impossible. With the barest of essentials, I quickly finished packing, rushed out the door with a headache worthy of a museum, flagged a cab, and hit the road with the slowest fucking cab driver in the tri-state area.

As traffic piled up around the Brooklyn-Battery Tunnel and four lanes merged into one, thoughts of heading home became less realistic. I would catch a later flight. No big deal. Simple *c'est la vie* reactions are easy to digest when you're unaware that the best flight of your life is waiting for you on the tarmac.

And then we were flying! Apparently, my old Asian driver had a little Dale Earnhardt Jr. in him and he honked and weaved his way through the tunnel to the open road of the expressway, pushing the limits of his four-banger Camry until we reached JFK with minutes to spare. Had I tipped him a million bucks, it still wouldn't have been enough. But hindsight is 20/20, and a twenty percent tip on fifty-two bucks was enough to make him smile.

-3-

Meanwhile, back at 35,000 feet, I wasn't smiling. I was struggling to find a diamond of dialogue in the rough that was my brain. Miss 18F and I had already covered so much ground—more ground than I'd covered with countless other girls on my journey through singledom—and I was running low on topics.

"So...uh...um...where did you live when you went to UCLA?"

Probably a C- on the scale of intriguing ways to lure her from the computer, but it was a passing grade and before long school was back in session. I knew West L.A. pretty well and we played the name game on places we'd been on Abbott Kinney: Hal's, Gjelina, Intelligentsia.

Tasty talk soon segued to her experience working as

the right-hand woman for a notorious Beverly Hills gallerist—a gallerist who had been on my curiosity list since I
heard horror stories about him back in grad school. And
while she didn't spill the whole can of beans, Miss 18F
gave me a nice bowl of art gossip to nosh on for a while.

Did I mention that this girl was amazing?

Anyway, common ground was obviously growing and
somewhere around Colorado we decided to treat ourselves
to a few beers—two cans of Blue Moon, to be precise. It
wasn't my idea. Frankly, the thought of anything alcoholic
entering my body made my heart skip. Still, I couldn't say
no.

As my beer grew less full, I spent less time reveling
in the complexity of her character and more time losing
myself in the simplicity of her beauty. The way her bangs
jetted across her forehead with a subtle curve that perfectly cropped the contours of her face. The cute mole on
the left side of her nose that drew me up to her soft brown
eyes, which shone like amber against the trickling hints of
cabin light. What a doll she was, what a doll.

In the back of my mind, I prayed the captain would
interrupt this moment of bliss only to inform us that LAX
was no more and that we would have to carry on to Hawaii.
Five more hours of paradise, followed by actual paradise,
would've been the perfect end to a perfect trip. But we had
already begun our descent.

Part of me wanted to slide into the middle seat, caress
her soft cheeks, and kiss her with the clichéd gusto you only
see in bad movies. However, when you meet someone as

undeniably wonderful as Miss 18F, you don't want to jeopardize your future for the fruits of an in-flight romance. If she's not on board, then you botch the landing. And I couldn't botch *this* landing. I'd never forgive myself. So I just stayed in my seat, cherishing the last drops of my Blue Moon, and watched as Los Angeles neared.

Soon the radiant glow of sunshine and smog began to cool our exchange. Visions of the lives we were returning to became too heavy to see past. She was coming home to L.A. to end a decade in residence and pack up for a new life in New York. I was coming home to come home. Two different paths that Hollywood execs in the studios below would surely love to sell as fantasy to the millions of dreamers desperately searching for Mr. or Mrs. Right in all the wrong places. But this fantasy was my reality and it was ending.

Or was it?

-4-

As the plane touched down and docked at our terminal, I turned to Miss 18F and confessed, "I think we're going to be friends *forever*."

Her face quickly lit up and she agreed. We both knew this flight was one in a million; maybe more. So we exchanged information and promised to meet up before she made her official move to New York the following week. It took a few days to coordinate, but on the eve of her departure we went to Venice Beach and shared a day so romantic it could only be interpreted as bragging—so I'll keep it short.

While we sat in the warm sand, Miss 18F asked me what I was doing all the way over *there*? I was only about an airplane seat away, but I guess she figured we weren't in the air anymore.

I asked her, "Is this the part where the guy gets to kiss the girl?"

Her eyes said yes, and so I moved toward her, caressed her soft cheeks, and finally kissed her with the clichéd gusto you only see in bad movies...and it was perfect.

Miss 18F on Venice Beach.

EATEN ALIVE

I was going jewelry shopping with the ladies. My matriarchal 94-year-old Grandma Patsy had spoiled my family with an all-expense paid trip to Hawaii for the holidays. It was New Year's Day 2011 and she wanted to head to the nearby town of Haleiwa to look for something pricey to add to her collection—and to buy my mom something nice, but less expensive.

The night before, some generous locals treated me to something more within my budget. I spent New Year's Eve drinking keg beer and doing crappy cocaine with my brother, Alex, at a raging party and had to walk five miles through the dark, spooky wilderness of Oahu's North Shore to get back to our hotel. I stumbled in with the morning shift employees around 4 a.m. and passed out on my giant bed, fully clothed.

Next thing I knew, the sun was up and I was in the Turtle Bay Hotel lobby waiting on a taxi with my grandma and my mom. My overindulgent brother hadn't come back from the party yet, so he was excused from daytime activities. And even though I tried my best to resemble a 'Do Not Disturb' door ornament, my mom deemed me fit for family activities.

Before our vehicle pulled up, I stepped aside to prep my nerves with a quick cigarette. As I puffed away, I noticed the waves breaking in front of the hotel. They were crystal-clear cylinders of surfing perfection—five feet high with not a breath of wind on them. It was then that I got an idea…a stupid one.

-2-

Since the day we arrived in Hawaii, the waves were *huge*. Massive swells traditionally pound the North Shore during the winter months, making some of the largest and most deadly waves in the world. This year was no exception. Twenty-foot sets relentlessly thrashed the local beaches, turning my would-be surf trip into a poolside cocktail retreat.

Back in southern California, I spent most of my life surfing considerably smaller waves, but I always longed to test my luck at the epicenter of the surfing world. My dream was to catch one wave at the Banzai Pipeline. For those of you not familiar with the Banzai Pipeline (a.k.a. Pipeline or Pipe), you most likely are. Its epic barreling waves have served as the backdrop for countless movies, TV shows, ad campaigns, surf contests, t-shirts, and other things surf-related. If the ocean is the Louvre, then Pipe-line is the Mona Lisa.

As much as I wanted to align myself with oceanic great-ness, my lack of technical, physical, and mental expertise was drowning my chances. Not that I was an aquatic inval-id; I competed on my high school surf team, and although I wasn't a bona fide ripper, I could hold my own amongst my peers. But a few scary experiences in larger surf made me realize that my balls weren't going to get any bigger and I was probably better suited for land activities like catching the flu.

Despite that, I never got sick of surfing, and my dream of riding Pipe was still posted on my bucket list some-where between playing for the Lakers and organizing my sock drawer. So when I saw the waves in front of the hotel had shrunk to a less-frightening size, I figured my dream was ready to come true.

-3-

The taxi dropped me off at Pipeline with my surfboard and continued on with my mom and grandma to Halei-wa. As I walked from the main highway toward the beach, I should've been shitting my shorts. Maybe it was because I was still legally drunk, but I felt surprisingly at ease. There was, however, something odd in the air. No roar from the waves smashing onto the coral reef; no birds screeching overhead; no people talking—the beach was silent.

I made my way onto the coarse sand and looked at

the ocean lineup. An incredible head-high barreling wave swept across the beach and spit a massive shower of spray into the closing face. The wave was empty. Now, in all the research I had done over the years, the one constant with Pipeline was that it was crowded...like Walmart-on-Black-Friday-in-the-ghetto crowded. Surfers came from all over the globe to fight with hundreds of daredevils for the chance to catch the best wave of their lives. But for some reason, on this early morning, the pecking order was down to just one chicken.

My godfather, John, lived in Hawaii in the late '70s and he told me about fluke days when he would score uncrowded Pipe. If the waves were too small for the big shots, or you timed it just right, you could pick off a few gems before the crowds clocked in. Maybe that was the case. The waves were not the size that experts would classify as ideal Pipeline. And since the majority of the local and visiting surfers attended the same crazy party I did, the likelihood of a hangover epidemic on the North Shore was quite likely.

With the conditions tailored to my perfection, I strapped on my leash and paddled out into the ocean. The convenient thing about Pipe is that it breaks pretty close to shore. Some surf spots on Hawaii are located on the other side of the horizon and require that thing called *energy*, which I was lacking, to get to. But 90 seconds into my paddle, I was in the perfect spot, ready to make my move.

On cue, a nice little nugget appeared on the horizon. With no one in my way, I swung around and paddled into what I imagined was the proper takeoff spot. I was wrong. In a heartbeat, the waved jacked up to a vertical wall of liquid brick and threatened to toss me toward the emergency room. I pulled back with all my beer-supplemented strength and avoided the wipeout, but now I was starting to think that at 5'8", I was better suited to slam-dunk on LeBron James than to catch a damn wave. Even dress socks would never kill me, no matter how poorly I paired them. Yet, there I was—smack dab in the fantasy I wanted, and I wanted out.

The easy solution would've been to paddle to shore and begin a two-hour walk of shame back to the hotel bar, but that brand of embarrassment wasn't on tap. The waves kept rolling in one after another, and they were getting bigger. Any sign of safe passage was lost as I clawed at the water, hoping to dodge the onslaught of crashing sea that was inches from my head. I pressed down on my board and slipped through the ocean while a ten-foot wave passed over me and took an inch off my hairline. When I finally popped to the surface like a turd in a punchbowl, I could feel the burn from a thousand Camel Lights scorching my lungs. I could taste the Kalua pork from last night melting in hot acid in my guts. But I couldn't see myself on shore. I was still in the ocean, in deep, but on the surface.

As the surf session from hangover hell continued with no end in sight, I knew I was either gonna have to catch a wave toward land or grow some gills. So, I took a few deep breaths and paddled for the smallest big wave I could find. A menacing seven-foot set was what I came up with and it sucked me up with more fervor than a horny whore. The second I hopped to my feet, I could sense the ocean forcing me down the steep face. It towered well over my head when I finally reached the bottom and made my backside turn. The hardest part was behind me, but something was wrong. My board began to wobble underneath me, which meant that my feet and surfboard were filing for divorce. With the jagged reef just inches below the surface, I fought to keep the odd couple together and locked my knees. My momentum shifted in my favor and I straightened out just in time for the pitching wave to cover my body in a tube of misty air. Absolute surfing perfection was achieved.

After the wave finally pinched shut and sent me to the safety of the shoulder, I arched my head to the heavens and closed my eyes. As I sunk slowly under the weight of my stunned carcass, I was ready to race to the hotel and tell my little brother why it pays to stop snorting drugs before sunrise. But before I could get to my stomach and paddle the final fifteen yards to shore, a swift jolt from below catapulted me off my board. When I fell back into the water, I thought for a moment that I had hit the reef. But reefs don't punch like that. An animal had hit me…a big one.

Amidst the sudden confusion, I had enough sense to survey my surroundings underwater. The rich salt water nearly blinded me and all I could see were blue splotches and brown blobs. Between the brown areas of reef, the aqua-blue water receded into darker marine hues. It was in the darker depths that I spotted a dark mass, neither blue nor brown, but gray with a white underside. I didn't need Lasiks to see that it wasn't a sardine. The best-case scenario was that it was Flipper with an eating disorder. Being a natural-born pessimist, I knew my luck had run out when I caught my perfect wave. And as the curious shape drew closer and its features came into focus, I knew it was a shark. Tiger, bull, or great white, I wasn't sure. That was for the coroners to decide. All I knew was it was bigger than me, and I was swimming in its kitchen.

Rather than roll over and play inedible, I hauled ass toward my board. It must've been an appetizing escape, because I didn't make it more than a few strokes before I was demoted from the top of the food chain. The shark chomped down on my right leg, sending a mushroom cloud of blood into my screaming face. I kept waving toward the surface, trying to break free, but the bastard wouldn't budge. Then a harsh crunch, followed by more blood, and a loud pop registered as the loss of my leg. Sadly, there was no time to get sentimental about appendages. I still had my dick, balls, heart, and head to preserve, *in that order*.

To make matters worse, the shark had severed my leg at the knee, which meant I wasn't bound to my surfboard anymore. So right when paralytic shock turned dog-paddling into an extreme sport, I had another handicap to deal with. The challenge got even lousier after I reached the surface and saw that I was further from land than before. In the midst of the attack, the monster must've dragged me into deeper waters where it was cool to make a mess. I tried to move, but my body and my mind had conflicting goals. Sink was triumphing over swim, which meant life was gonna lose to death before I ever got to test-drive a peg leg.

As more blood drained from my stump and my tools for buoyancy crapped out, I took one final breath then dipped below the surface. Through the murky mess of blue splotches, brown blobs, and bloody haze, I noticed my gray & white leg thief. He was ten feet away and gaining on the rest of his breakfast. I didn't even bother to guard my goods when he wrapped his enormous jaws around my head. What good was my dick without my head, really? I could never make it as a dildo. I was apparently destined to be shark shit.

In a few moments, my head would be torn from my chest and I would begin a quick trip down the shark's rugged mouth, past rows of razor-sharp teeth, and through some pinkish horizontal throat that looked like grade-F vagina. I thought my whole life was set to flash before my eyes. One last look at all the glorious events that defined my short, sweet time on earth. But all I could hear was my name.

"Adam...Adam! *Adam! Adaaaaammmmm!*"

-4-

When I woke up, my brother was standing at the edge of my bed, yanking on my right foot, and it was still attached to my body. He looked *worse* than grade-F vagina.

"*Adam!* Where's your Advil? I feel like I'm going to die."

I wanted to hug him to death for saving me from my nightmare, but I did the kinder thing and handed him two pills from my bedside drawer. The poor kid had just walked the same five-mile stretch of island under the heat of the morning sun while coming down on twice as much drugs and alcohol as me. He threw back the pills and collapsed on his bed.

"Hey, we're supposed to go shopping with Mom and Grandma pretty soon," I said.

He was already snoring. Of course, I was too startled to fall back asleep, so I headed out to the balcony and had a smoke. I smiled when I saw the waves in front of the hotel. They were still twenty feet tall and nasty.

Mom, Grandma Patsy, and me on vacation.

A DATE WITH A DOMINATRIX

-1-

When you first meet a nice girl, you never expect that one day she will tie up your genitals with a shoelace and mercilessly pull you around your bedroom while calling you a pussy.

I encountered Lyra at a concert when I randomly sat next to her and bummed a cigarette. She was 21 years old, cute with slim legs, and she had three nose rings, which I diagnosed as repetitive emblems of faux rebellion. Lyra was the kind of girl that probably worked at Hot Topic, or American Apparel by way of Hot Topic.

Whomever her assumed employer, it didn't take long for her to ask me what I did for work. Thankfully, my art career was developing into something that strangers might not perceive as pathetic. I recently had one of my paintings featured on a billboard in Los Angeles, received a favorable amount of press, and was revving up for my second major solo exhibition. So, upon her inquiry, I decided to forego the humble route and go into total brag mode to see what it might do for my hibernating sex life. It just so happened that she knew of my art. Thanks to the divine power of Instagram, Lyra had scrolled upon my billboard and thought it was really cool.

"I gotta get your number!" she said.

Like so many pompous douchebags before me, I hooked a girl by name-dropping myself. It was a new-found treat to be the unquestionable alpha, the subject of desire of the more desirable physical specimen. Lyra and I swapped information and could've swapped more that evening, but she had a needy tagalong friend who wanted to head home early and I was a little too drunk to pull off an amicable kidnapping.

-2-

A few weeks later, we began our first date at a dive bar near my apartment in Echo Park called Little Joy. Old rock-abilly music blasted while hipsters hung around a dark room that was a shade brighter than pitch black. Lyra's flowing blonde hair lit the way as we moved toward two empty stools at the bar and commenced with a stiff round of vodka drinks. The liquor helped ease any initial awkwardness and playful banter flowed smoothly between us until Lyra's phone started vibrating. She glanced down at the screen then not-so-nonchalantly slipped her cracked iPhone inside her purse.

"Oh, it's just work e-mails," Lyra said.

I didn't ask, I thought to myself.

Immediately, the air between us grew stale. Was it an ex-boyfriend? A *current* boyfriend? Again, I didn't ask or really care. The main ingredient in any 21-year-old is drama. But being a mature adult, I gave her a chance to look like she wasn't lying.

"So, I forgot to ask when we first met...what is it that you do for work?"

Her mouth began to tense up, as if her chin were a slug and my words were salt.

"I mean, I notice that you post a lot of pictures of rescue animals. Do you work at an animal shelter?"

Lyra's face softened, then morphed into a smirk.

"Well, there are cages where I work."

I was stumped. She could tell.

"Can I be honest with you, Adam?"

Our first date and honesty was already up for debate. I nodded, then she opened up her mouth and annunciated the following résumé filler.

"I'm a professional dominatrix."

I almost fell off my stool.

"You're not creeped out, are you?" she asked.

"No! In fact, this might be the most interesting first date I've ever had," I replied, and I meant it.

"That's awesome! Most guys can't really handle what I do for a living."

And that's when it hit me. In the millions of minutes of pornography I'd watched, I didn't learn anything about dominatrices beyond whips and leather fetish wear. Torture was something that women did to me when I wasn't being pleasured.

"Well, I know it's a very taboo profession, but what's a typical day in the life of an aspiring dominatrix?"

"I guess it all depends," she said. "Some days I like to humiliate guys while they massage my feet. Other days I like to fuck them in the ass with big black dildos."

Again, I don't know how the hell I didn't fall off my stool. This time, I think my eyes bulged out of my head and acted as anti-gravity balls. This girl was not the Hot Topic employee I predicted. Lyra was someone who could crush a presidential campaign in one shift. And even though I was far from a curious client, I was intrigued beyond belief.

"Can we please go someplace quieter where I can listen to you talk?"

The growing crowd and thumping music were threatening to muffle dialogue I might not hear again in several lifetimes, so I paid our tab and we walked up Sunset Boulevard to a bar with better acoustics.

-3-

After ordering more vodka, Lyra and I congregated at a padded bench where two happy couples were seated on opposite sides of us. There, she told me all about the colorful clients that frequented her dungeon in downtown L.A.: the ex-rock star who liked to have cigarettes ashed in his mouth, the famous screenwriter who loved to drink her urine, the cross-dressing high school coach who enjoyed

sucking her strap-on cock, the old Persian man that preferred to dress up like a baby and be fed nitrous oxide
until he passed out, the tough black dude who wanted to
be kicked in the balls for hours at a time, and the airline
steward who used to lock his dick in a tiny chastity box so
he wouldn't get a hard-on but recently underwent an irre-
versible operation that prevented him from ever getting an
erection.

As Lyra happily boasted about these gentlemen, I
noticed the couples around us—who likely met on Tinder
and were having trouble discussing gluten-free lifestyle
choices—began moving farther down the bench. They
may have been getting ear infections from Lyra's gross
banter, but I was pressed firmly against her thigh, waiting
with curious delight for every sentence that spewed from
her filthy mouth. Maybe it was my sincere interest in her
job. Likely it was the alcohol. Regardless, I was so turned
on by the novelty of being near someone so fearless that I
couldn't wait to have sex with her. There was just one question I had to ask before I put my health in the hands of the
Evel Knievel of sex.

"Forgive me if I'm out of line, but do you have *inter-
course* with your clients?"

"Hell no! I do all the fucking. I don't even have to take
my clothes off."

"That's a relief! So how much do these dudes pay you
to not fuck them?"

"A couple hundred bucks an hour."

She was starting to sound like marriage material. I

pounded the rest of my cocktail to sober my shell-shocked brain, then I checked the time on my phone. The bar was closing in a few minutes and I knew we both didn't want to finish our date.

"Do you want to head to my place to continue this conversation?" I asked.

Lyra's left eyebrow hiked up a tad.

"Of course!" she said.

-4-

Shortly after arriving at my apartment, Lyra and I began making out on a crappy Ikea couch in my living room. The upside to having uncomfortable furniture is that you can suggest going to your bedroom with little fuss from the ladies. Once our mouths reconvened on my bed and articles of clothing began to appear on the floor, a pressing issue surfaced in my mind.

"Lyra, I just want you to know that I'm into exploring some new sexual things, but I don't want anything done to me that will require a trip to the emergency room. I have some work to do in the morning."

"Okay. I'll ease into things."

"Sounds good. Oh, and don't shove anything in this room up my butt, please."

"Well, you're no fun!"

"Use your imagination elsewhere."

I would soon regret those words, but at the time Lyra was straddling my chest with her smooth thighs and I was making eye contact with her perky c-cups and her cleanly shaved cha-cha. When I reached up to reacquaint myself with a twenty-one-year-old boob for the first time since my twenties, I didn't realize what I was in for.

"I didn't say you could touch my tits," Lyra snarled.

After four hours of bragging about her advanced sexual tolerance, Lyra threw me out at second base. I hoped she was kidding. Her tone told me she wasn't. I dropped my hand down as directed, but it happened to land on the contour of her rump.

"And you don't get to touch my ass unless I say so!"

In a flash, she seized my hand and pinned it forcefully above my head.

"Okay, Lyra."

"Yes, *Mistress* Lyra!" she ordered.

"Yes, Mistress Lyra!" I replied.

The unquestionable alpha title was hers and I figured I should play along if I was going to extract any pleasure from her naked body.

"So, what can I touch?"

"What can I touch, *Mistress Lyra*?"

"Yeah, sorry. First timer. My bad."

I took a deep breath, then tried to swallow my sarcasm and act the part of her target audience—a submissive pervert with more issues than a newsstand.

"What can I do to please you, Mistress Lyra?"

"Well, actually, you *can* rub my ass because it feels good. I just want you to know the rules."

Lyra spun around, flaunting her succulent cheeks.

After I carefully placed my palms upon the warm mounds, she instructed that I spank her. This was a technique I thoroughly researched at Porn University and utilized for years. I pulled back my right hand with my fingers spread apart and swiftly laid into the flesh. A crisp snap echoed throughout my tiny bedroom—the resonance of a perfect landing.

"What the fuck was *that*?" Lyra groaned.

"Hey, I'm just following orders, Mistress Lyra."

"That was *not* how you slap an ass."

Lyra grabbed my hand, pushed my fingers into a closed paddle shape, then swung my hand firmly into her ass so that it landed with all my weight flush against the surface. A thicker snap, almost like a thud, filled the room, followed by a moan.

"That's better," she said.

Evidently, my pornographic mentors gave amateur ass slaps. I practiced a few more times on each cheek until Lyra felt like moving on to a new subject. She spun back around and began flicking my nipples with her tongue until the meaty centers raised up. Then she ran her tongue down my chest to the head of my cock and repeated the gesture until it too raised up. From there, she extended her pointy mouth muscle up and down the length of my hard-on.

"You like that, don't you?" Lyra purred.

"Oh, yes, Mistress Lyra."

I closed my eyes. Heaven began to appear amidst the darkness. And that's when Satan fired back. Lyra flicked my nuts with her index finger like she was trying to launch a cigarette butt over a mountain. A bolt of nauseating energy exploded in my stomach. My body heaved forward as my knees mimicked a closing bear trap. Lyra pushed me down on the bed, regaining control of her flailing victim.

"Oh, you poor baby!" she snickered.

"Hey, you don't have balls! You have no idea how bad that feels, Mistress Lyra!"

"If you act like you're in pain, I'm only going to make it worse."

"If you flick my balls again, I'm gonna puke on you and send you home without a shower, so flick something else."

Her eyebrow hiked up, again. I knew I was fucked without getting laid. Sure enough, she moved her hand up my penis and flicked me square in the helmet. The pain was immense, but it was a vacation compared to the previous finger blast. I barely squirmed. Lyra did it again, and again, and again, and I squirmed, and again, and I yelled.

"All right, you made your point, Mistress Lyra!"

My deflating dick also notified her of my dwindling interest. She countered by spreading her legs across my thighs and opening her pussy enough to locate her clit, which she massaged while she watched me watch. My cock couldn't stay mad and rocketed back into form. Amused, Lyra spit onto her palm and started stroking my weakest link with her free hand. This game of two-hand touch continued until I felt an orgasm brewing in my wounded balls. Typically, I wouldn't waste my climax on heated foreplay, but I thought the way this night was unfolding, this might be dessert.

"I'm gonna cum!" I proclaimed.

Immediately, Lyra's hand was not around my penis. It was wrapped around my throat. Lyra stared into my eyes, past my skull, and into my brain. Her look was crazed.

"*I didn't say you could cum!*"

"I'm sorry, Mistress Lyra, but if you tug on me long enough, eventually I'll explode."

She giggled and her flaming irises returned to their natural green color.

"Are we done, Mistress Lyra?"

"Does the poor little baby want to quit? I promise I'll make it better."

She was baiting me. The cynic inside me believed this would surely lead to more bad things. Each of Lyra's sexy gestures was followed by pain, which meant I'd have to endure another obstacle if I were to end on a high note. She started caressing my face—the part where the jaw meets the ear: the j-spot. I took the bait.

"Fine. Continue, Mistress Lyra."

She began to take stock of my room.

"Do you have any rope?"

"No." I said, but knew damn well there was some in my kitchen drawer.

"That's all right."

Lyra hopped off the bed, grabbed her blue Vans high-top sneaker and began quickly removing the shoelace. The referees at Foot Locker couldn't debone a shoe that fast. My pulse grew heavier as I pondered what she intended to do with such a thing. It was too short to tie my arms or legs. It would make a lousy mouth gag. I wasn't wearing a loose shoe.

Lyra returned to bed with the shoelace and went straight for my balls.

"Wait, wait, waaaaaaaaaiiit a second! I think we're officially done here!"

"Don't you trust me?"

"I trust that you're fucking crazy."

"Let me rephrase that. I'm a professional, Adam. I train with people that have done this for many years. I know what I'm doing. And I haven't been with a guy I like in a really long time, and I like you. So please don't worry."

She sounded trustworthy—probably how serial killers sound before they chop up their lovers.

"Fine, but this is the last trick."

"Just relax," she said, then made a firm loop around the base of my balls and tied another loop around the base of my cock. Next, she ran equal parts of the shoelace in a fence-like pattern up my shaft and made one more firm loop below the head of my penis. Lyra used the remaining few inches of the shoelace as a leash, which she used to move my poor dick as she pleased. The tightness of the material concerned me, but the ease with which Lyra manipulated the shoelace validated her experience, so I let her continue. After the design was finished, Lyra slid down and began licking the exposed flesh on my dick until I was rock hard. Sadly, the shoelace was applied at a more limp status and my middle member began to swell.

"Hey, I think you put this on too tightly, Mistress Lyra."

"Stop your whining!"

Lyra yanked the leash and pulled me out of bed. We were both on our feet, eye-to-eye, when she began leading me around the room. Maybe she thought I'd start barking, but she was the real animal, posing as a human, searching for prey. I glanced down at the penis in her possession. It was bloated and purple like a jellyfish caught in a net.

"I told you I didn't want to go to the emergency room!"

"Relax! I've seen guys' dicks get big and turn black and they lived."

"Well, if mine turned into a big black dick that would be fine, but all I see is a scared white dick and it's freaking me out!"

"Don't be such a pussy!"

The man who was twelve years her senior was just a girl in Lyra's crazy world. I sensed an uncomfortable numbness foreclose on my favorite dermal property as the skin continued to balloon.

"Lyra, the show's over! *Fuckin' untie me, right now!*"

Her fervor dampened at the roar of my demand and she untied me. I nervously watched until my penis deflated into a passable version of its former self.

"I'm gonna go to bed. On top of the work I have to do in the morning, I think I need to find a therapist."

We shared a laugh. Mine was marred by disgust. I collapsed onto my full-sized mattress and shrunk into the fetal position.

"I promised you I'd make it better," Lyra said, then snuggled up to me.

I didn't acknowledge her presence and shut my eyes, praying that Hell would reclaim her. Once again, Lyra visited my genitals to lobby for an erection. She pushed me on my back, straddled my waist, and began grinding her pubic bone against my goods. As expected, One-Eyed Willy rose from the dead.

"See. He's not mad at me."

"He likes my left hand just as much. Don't flatter yourself."

Lyra fed off my verbal jab and motioned for a kiss. I reverse puckered, successfully blocking her affection. When she pulled away, the words, "Get the fuck out of my house!" were on the tip of my tongue. I opened my mouth, ready to end the madness, when Lyra proved that she was true to her word. She slid my wounded cock inside her cozy vagina and made everything better. The missionary position was scandalous from that day forth. It was also the place where I felt a real connection to Lyra. After so much mismatched struggle, our bodies complemented one another beautifully. I thought, *I could get used to this.* Obviously, I might die in the process of getting back there again, but for a few glorious minutes, Lyra and I were one. We locked lips and passed our breaths back and forth as I moved closer to a proper orgasm. Would my testicles still work? It didn't matter. No shoelace could hold back the passion I planned to unload on Lyra. So I thrust into her— eyes locked, no madness, only desire—until an eruption appeared imminent. One more push of passionate synergy and...

"That's all for tonight, Adam."

Lyra slid off my fully charged genitals and gathered her clothes from the floor.

"Wait! You can't...what just...*huh*?"

Lyra looked at me as if I were her masterpiece. It took a purple penis, but she had crafted the ultimate sculpture of blue balls. She dressed quickly and didn't bother to lace up her shoe as she left my apartment without saying another word. I began to laugh uncontrollably. Why couldn't I meet a nice girl who was actually a nice girl? Somehow, I knew I wouldn't enjoy the gentle alternative.

Life keeps punishing me with good stories.

Mistress Lyra (photo by Michael Vegas).

ACKNOWLEDGMENTS

Special thanks to Tommy, Brynne, Seth, Rachel, Angie, Russ, Piper, Walt, the Hagstroms, Team Hip Hop, Miss 18F, Bah-Bah, Brian, Kit, Cody, Bret, Kelsey, Jordan, Sharon, the Brunswicks, Ron, Ryan, Lonny, Rooz, Tyler, Kelly, Nick, Edgar, Matt, Mikey, Aaron, Carl, Michael Vegas, DMTina & the Bumps, the Growlers crew, and all of the people that helped inspire this book...Even the guy who punched me in the face.

ABOUT THE AUTHOR

Adam Mars was born in southern California. His artwork has been featured in the *Los Angeles Times, Los Angeles Magazine, LA Weekly,* and other publications. He lives and works in Los Angeles. *Unreal for Real* is his first collection of stories.

Made in the USA
Monee, IL
26 December 2022

19473221R00114